In For the Kill

A Thriller

Derek Benfield

A Samuel French Acting Edition

SAMUELFRENCH.COM
SAMUELFRENCH-LONDON.CO.UK

Copyright © 1981 by Derek Benfield
All Rights Reserved
IN FOR THE KILL is fully protected under the copyright laws of the United States of America, the British Commonwealth, including Canada, and all other countries of the Copyright Union. All rights, including professional and amateur stage productions, recitation, lecturing, public reading, motion picture, radio broadcasting, television and the rights of translation into foreign languages are strictly reserved.

ISBN 978-0-573-11180-8

www.SamuelFrench.com
www.SamuelFrench-London.co.uk

FOR PRODUCTION ENQUIRIES

UNITED STATES AND CANADA
Info@SamuelFrench.com
1-866-598-8449

UNITED KINGDOM AND EUROPE
Plays@SamuelFrench-London.co.uk
020-7255-4302

Each title is subject to availability from Samuel French, depending upon country of performance. Please be aware that *IN FOR THE KILL* may not be licensed by Samuel French in your territory. Professional and amateur producers should contact the nearest Samuel French office or licensing partner to verify availability.

CAUTION: Professional and amateur producers are hereby warned that *IN FOR THE KILL* is subject to a licensing fee. Publication of this play does not imply availability for performance. Both amateurs and professionals considering a production are strongly advised to apply to Samuel French before starting rehearsals, advertising, or booking a theatre. A licensing fee must be paid whether the title is presented for charity or gain and whether or not admission is charged.

The professional rights in this play are controlled by The Agency, 24 Pottery Lane, Holland Park, London W11 4LZ.

No one shall make any changes in this title for the purpose of production. No part of this book may be reproduced, stored in a retrieval system, or transmitted in any form, by any means, now known or yet to be invented, including mechanical, electronic, photocopying, recording, videotaping, or otherwise, without the prior written permission of the publisher. No one shall upload this title, or part of this title, to any social media websites.

For all enquiries regarding motion picture, television, and other media rights, please contact Samuel French.

CHARACTERS

Paula
Frank
James
Mark
Susan

The action takes place in Paula and James's home in the suburbs of a big city

ACT I	Scene 1	A Friday evening in summer
	Scene 2	Saturday, late afternoon
	Scene 3	An hour later
ACT II	Scene 1	Two hours later
	Scene 2	The next morning

Time—the present

Other plays by DEREK BENFIELD:

Beyond A Joke
Caught On The Hop
Panic Stations
A Bird In The Hand
Murder For The Asking
Off The Hook
Post Horn Gallop
Fish Out Of Water
Running Riot
Wild Goose Chase

ACT I

Scene 1

The sitting-room of Paula and James's comfortable house on the outskirts of a big city. A pleasant Friday evening in the summer

The front door opens directly into the sitting-room and you descend three steps to the floor level. On the other side of the room French windows lead out on to a paved patio and the pleasant garden. A door up C *leads out to the rest of the house. There is a sofa with a table above it, an armchair with a small table beside it and a desk against the wall below the windows. The telephone is on the desk. A drinks table is* L *of the windows, and a small table with flowers is down* L. *There are bookshelves in a recess in the wall above the front door with a stereo and speakers. The furniture and decoration is tasteful and expensive*

When the CURTAIN *rises the room is empty. A transistor radio on the armchair table is blasting out: apparently without a listener. After a moment the doorbell rings: sharply. The radio takes no notice. A disc jockey prattles into the next hit melody: but quieter music this time, more romantic. Again the doorbell rings. With the music now less strident the bell can be heard by Paula, who is in the bathroom. She comes in to answer it, a bit flustered. He is early*

Paula is an attractive woman in her thirties. She is wearing a glamorous dressing-gown and has not quite finished doing her hair. And gentlemen arriving to collect her when she has not finished her hair is not what she likes. She wonders whether to finish it off and keep him waiting or not. The bell rings again. She is not too pleased

Paula All right. Just a minute. I'm coming . . .! (*She goes and opens the door*)

Frank is standing there. He is a pleasant man in his late forties

She is surprised to see a stranger there and is rather nonplussed for a moment

Oh.
Frank Sorry. Did I . . . ?
Paula I was just doing my hair.
Frank I didn't get you out of the bath, did I?
Paula Does it look as bad as all that?
Frank Oh, no! No. I didn't mean . . . It looks very nice, as a matter of fact.
Paula You don't *have* to say that. I was just finishing it off. I'm going out.
Frank (*disappointed*) Oh . . .

Paula Actually, I thought you were . . .
Frank Your date? (*He smiles*) I'm sorry.
Paula There's no need to be.
Frank I mean—for me. Not being your date.

Paula likes being flattered and smiles in spite of her fluster

Paula He's not in, I'm afraid.
Frank What?
Paula Oh—excuse me. I'll turn this off.

She goes to turn off the radio so that they can talk more easily. As she does so he comes in and closes the door behind him. She turns and sees him inside and looks a little surprised

(*Gently sarcastic*) Do come in.
Frank Oh, I *am* sorry. Look, I . . .
Paula Do you spend all your life apologizing?
Frank Only when I've upset someone.
Paula You haven't upset me.
Frank Oh, good. (*He comes down the steps into the room*)
Paula Just surprised me, that's all. Coming in like that.
Frank What time are you expecting him?
Paula Who?
Frank Your—date.
Paula Any moment. When you rang I thought . . . (*As if she felt an explanation was needed*) He's an old friend.

He smiles, looking directly at her

Frank Yes. I'm sure he is.

A moment. She is not sure what he means

Paula James isn't here, I'm afraid. So if you like to leave your name, I'll tell him you . . .
Frank Frank.
Paula All right, Frank. I'll tell him. Now I really must finish getting ready . . .

He goes to her

Frank You needn't bother.
Paula Well, I can't go out in this, can I? I must change. So if you'll forgive me . . . (*She makes a move hopefully*)
Frank I meant you needn't bother to tell him.

She stops

Paula Isn't it important, then?
Frank H'm?
Paula What you wanted to see my husband about. (*In sudden doubt*) You *are* a friend of James, aren't you?
Frank Oh, yes. Yes. We've known each other—a long time.

Act I, Scene 1

Paula (*politely*) I would ask you to wait, but I'm not expecting him back until much later.
Frank No, of *course* you aren't.

She looks puzzled

Paula You *knew* that?

He shrugs

Frank Well, I—I assumed.
Paula Assumed?
Frank When you thought I was your date.

She holds his look, not sure of his meaning

Paula (*a little coldly*) Her name's Valerie.
Frank Your . . . ?
Paula Yes.
Frank Oh, then I shouldn't worry about your hair. It's already *far* too good for Valerie.

Paula breaks away. He smiles understandingly

You did talk about "him" just now, you know. Oh, you needn't worry. I won't tell James. I *can* keep a secret.
Paula (*a little defensively*) It *isn't* a secret.
Frank Oh?

A pause, as they look at each other. Then Paula goes to him

Paula Look, you really must go now . . .
Frank Do you mind if I have a drink?

Paula looks rather taken aback

Paula Well, I . . .
Frank Gin would do very nicely.
Paula But I can't . . .
Frank Not too much tonic.
Paula I said I *can't*!
Frank Don't tell me James has drunk all the gin? Never mind. Anything'll do.
Paula (*smiling reasonably*) I really can't. I have to get dressed.
Frank Well, carry on! I can sit here sipping my drink and we can shout at each other through the door.
Paula And what would James say if he came back early?

Frank smiles

Frank He won't. He's gone to a meeting.

A pause

Paula How do *you* know?

He looks at her directly

Frank He told me.
Paula So—so you knew all the time that he wasn't going to be here?

He smiles guiltily

Frank Yes. As a matter of fact, I did.

She looks at him, puzzled but not yet alarmed. The telephone rings. She looks relieved

Paula That may be him now. Then you can have a word with him. (*She goes to answer the telephone*) Hullo . . .? (*It is not James*) Oh, it's you. For heaven's sake where are you? It's after half-past seven . . . What? . . . Yes, I—I know that, but . . . Well, of course I'm ready!

Frank smiles

Well, get here as quick as you can. (*She replaces the receiver, not at all pleased*)

He looks at her with a twinkle

Frank Valerie?
Paula He's been held up.
Frank Ah. So *he* won't be arriving just yet either?
Paula He said he'd hurry.
Frank And I'm sure he will. But now at least there's no panic, is there? Plenty of time for hair and dressing and all that. You might even have time to give me a drink.

She looks at him thoughtfully for a moment. Then smiles

Paula Oh. All right. (*She goes to the drinks*) Will vodka and tonic do?
Frank Even better than gin. (*He wanders below the sofa looking about*)

She pours two drinks. There is quite a pause

Paula How long have you known James?
Frank How long have *you* known Valerie?

She hesitates; but only for a second. Then they both smile

Paula I asked my question first.
Frank Twenty years.
Paula When he was married to Lisa.
Frank Yes.

She gives him his drink

Thanks. Cheers!
Paula Cheers.

They drink. She moves away towards the armchair

Frank We formed a company together.
Paula H'm?
Frank Making boxes.

Act I, Scene 1

Paula (*amused*) Boxes?
Frank Oh, there's a big demand for them, you know.
Paula I suppose there would be, yes. (*She sits on the arm of the chair*) Boxes?
Frank Yes. Quite a roaring trade we did for a while. Then we had what I think is known as a "cash flow problem". After that we went our seperate ways. I went to Australia for a while and we lost track of each other. (*He sits on the sofa*)
Paula But now you've met up again. Old chums reunion.
Frank (*with a smile*) Something like that. He hasn't changed a bit, you know.
Paula (*with a slight edge*) Except that *now* he's married to *me*.

He looks at her

Frank Yes. Now he's married to you. (*A brief pause*) How long have you . . . ?
Paula Been married?
Frank Yes.
Paula Two years.
Frank And already you're going out with "Valerie"?

Paula does not like this joke any more. She gets up and moves away

Paula Shall we stop calling him Valerie now, if you don't mind?
Frank Well, I don't know his real name, do I?
Paula (*firmly*) No. You don't. (*She is beginning to feel a little uneasy*) Why did you come here to see James when you knew he was at a meeting?
Frank I don't think I said I'd come to see James, did I?

She turns to look at him

Paula Well, naturally, I assumed . . .
Frank Everyone who comes here doesn't come to see James, surely? That wouldn't be very flattering, would it? Hordes of people arriving here and all to see James.

She smiles

I shouldn't think "Valerie" comes to see James very often . . .

She stops smiling

Well, if *you* go on being secretive, *I* shall have to go on calling him Valerie.
Paula I wasn't being secretive.
Frank Oh. I must have misunderstood.
Paula Mark.
Frank I see.
Paula (*defensively*) He's very nice.
Frank Yes. I'm sure he is.
Paula (*pointedly*) A very good friend.
Frank Of the family.

Paula Yes.

He looks directly at her. She moves away to avoid his eyes

You still haven't explained why you *didn't* come here to see James.

He looks at her innocently

Frank Oh. Haven't you realized?

She turns

Paula What? Realized what?
Frank I've come to see *you*.

Paula is beginning to feel apprehensive

Paula But I've never met you before.
Frank Does that matter?
Paula Well, I . . .
Frank I wouldn't have thought that mattered. Do you mind if I have another vodka? Or would that be going too far?
Paula (*abruptly*) Well, you'll have to help yourself. I've got to get dressed. Mark will be here any minute. (*She puts her glass down on the drinks table*)
Frank (*with a smile*) And we don't want to give him the wrong impression, do we? You know how people talk.

Paula gives him a patient look and goes off to the bedrooms

Left alone, Frank remains absolutely still for a moment, then he gets up thoughtfully and goes to refill his drink. He looks about the room, takes out a small cigar and is about to light it

Paula (*off*) There are cigarettes on the table.

He smiles at her psychic powers

Frank (*calling*) Thank you. I prefer cigars. (*Pause*) Is that all right?
Paula (*off*) What?
Frank (*calling*) Is it all right if I smoke a small cigar?
Paula (*off*) Smoke what the hell you like.
Frank (*calling*) Thanks.

Frank lights his cigar and goes across to the window thoughtfully. He goes outside and looks around for a moment as if studying the geography of the house. Then he comes back inside and carefully closes the doors to the garden. He wanders a little with his drink and cigar, looking about. He spots a photograph of Susan in a frame on the desk. He picks it up and looks at it

Paula returns. She has changed into an extremely nice dress

He gazes at her, obviously impressed. There is a pause as he looks at her in silence

Paula What's the matter?

Act I, Scene 1

Frank (*softly*) You look—beautiful.

She smiles, enjoying his flattery, though a little embarrassed by it

Paula Thank you.
Frank Really beautiful . . .

To escape his eyes she goes to collect her drink. He looks down at the photograph again. Paula notices that the windows have been closed and looks a little apprehensive, then she sees him looking at the photograph

Paula That's Susan. James's daughter.
Frank Yes. I know.

Paula moves edgily away

Paula Of course. I must remember. *You* knew him the first time around, didn't you?

He tries to smooth her feathers with flattery

Frank She's—not as pretty as her new mother.
Paula Stepmother.

He looks at her with a smile

Frank Is that how you think of yourself?
Paula It's what I am.

Frank looks at the photograph again

Frank I suppose you see her quite often?
Paula (*uninterestedly*) She stays here occasionally.
Frank James was always very fond of her.

Paula is not too enthusiastic

Paula Well, she's a clever girl. Kind to animals and liberally sprinkled with "O" levels.

He makes no comment, but quietly puts the photograph down again. She watches him for a moment, then comes towards him resolutely

Look, I *am* going out this evening . . .
Frank But he hasn't arrived yet.
Paula He'll be here any minute.
Frank We can't be sure of *that*, can we?

Paula is stopped in her tracks

Paula What?
Frank We can't be *sure* that he's going to arrive, can we?

A brief pause

Paula Whatever do you mean?
Frank Well, we can never be *sure* of anything. At least, *I* can't. But perhaps you're different.

Paula tries to reassure herself

Paula He's on his way. I know that. So whatever it is you came here to talk to me about, you'd better say it now while you've got the chance.

The telephone rings. A pause. He lifts the receiver and holds it out to her. Paula goes and takes it from him. He moves away

(*On the telephone*) Yes? ... What? ... Well, where the hell are you? (*She sighs impatiently as the caller rattles on*) Well, leave the bloody car and grab a taxi! (*She slams down the receiver*)

Frank smiles, gently remonstrating

Frank Ah—now you've upset Valerie.

She is not sure for a second whether she is going to be angry, then relaxes and laughs, moving towards the sofa

Paula His bloody car's broken down.
Frank Can't he put it right?
Paula To Mark, whatever goes on under the bonnet of a car is like the Sphinx—a total mystery!
Frank He'd better go to evening classes.
Paula (*with a smile*) Yes.
Frank I suppose James is better at that sort of thing?
Paula Yes ... (*She sits on the sofa. There is a moment's silence. Feeling slightly apprehensive, she tries to make conversation*) Are *you* married?
Frank Yes.
Paula You make that sound like the end of the conversation.

He moves towards her

Frank Oh, no. No. She's very nice. I'm extremely fond of her. We get on very well.
Paula But it's not exactly passionate?
Frank (*defensively*) I didn't say that.

She smiles at him provocatively, summing him up. He lowers his eyes

No. It's not exactly passionate. But I *do* know what goes on under the bonnet of a car.

They laugh

Paula Any children?
Frank Oh, yes. I know how to do *that*, as well!
Paula (*smiling*) I had a feeling you might. Well, I shall know who to come to now, won't I?
Frank (*with a laugh*) I *beg* your pardon?

She realizes what she has said and laughs

Paula When my car breaks down!

He pretends to be disappointed

Act I, Scene 1 9

Frank Ah. I was *afraid* that was what you meant.

She smiles at him approvingly

Paula You'd better be careful. Walking into other men's houses and flirting with their wives.
Frank (*in mock alarm*) Yes! James has probably got the place bugged. Recording every word.
Paula Good heavens—he wouldn't do that, surely?

Frank looks at her steadily

Frank Well, if he *does* he'll know all about Mark, won't he? (*He puts out his cigar in the ashtray on the sofa table*)

The light atmosphere between them ends as quickly as it started. Paula watches him thoughtfully as he wanders away, then tries to keep the polite conversation going

Paula How many?
Frank H'm?
Paula Children.
Frank Oh. Just one.
Paula Boy?
Frank Girl.
Paula Pretty?
Frank Very.
Paula How old is she?

A pause. He looks down

Frank (*quietly*) She—died, I'm afraid.

Paula is genuinely sorry

Paula Oh, dear. I am sorry. I—I didn't know.
Frank How could you? (*Reassuringly*) Oh, it's all right. Don't you worry. Long time ago now. I'm afraid I've drunk my vodka rather quickly.
Paula Then you'd better have another one.
Frank Thanks. (*He goes to help himself. Joking*) Y'know, if Mark doesn't turn up soon *I* may have to take you out to dinner.
Paula What would your wife say?
Frank I wouldn't tell her, would I?

They laugh. He moves to her with his drink

Paula Well, I must say, I'm very flattered.
Frank H'm?
Paula You coming here to-night when you knew James was at a meeting just so you could flirt with me.
Frank Oh, I didn't come here for that.
Paula (*disappointed*) You didn't?

He smiles

Frank Well, not *just* for that.

A pause

Paula Then what *did* you come here for?
Frank Well, as a matter of fact—I came about James.

Paula rises, alarmed

Paula He's all right, isn't he? I thought you said he was at a meeting. Nothing's happened to him, has it?
Frank Oh, no. No. He's quite all right. (*A brief pause*) At the *moment* . . .

A pause. She looks at him steadily, bewildered, sensing the change of atmosphere

Paula I—I don't know what you mean.
Frank (*presently*) Do you suppose he knows?
Paula Knows what?
Frank (*coldly*) About *you*.

A moment. Paula is now starting to feel nervous

Paula I wish I knew what you were talking about . . .
Frank (*loudly, ruthlessly*) Oh, come on! Mark isn't the *first*, is he?

Her anger mounting, Paula puts down her drink with a thump on the sofa table and faces him icily

Paula I think you'd better go. *Now!*
Frank (*reasonably*) But I'm trying to help you.
Paula (*pointing to the door*) Get out!

He continues inexorably, moving towards her

Frank Do you suppose James knows about Mark—and all the others?
Paula Now, look here . . . !
Frank (*strongly*) Don't let's waste time! You said Mark would be here in a minute. (*He puts his empty glass down on the sofa table*)

Paula does not know what to make of him, and cannot think what he is up to. She retreats a little

Paula Get out of here!
Frank But you still haven't answered my question. Do you suppose James knows about Mark and all the others? Well, he might, mightn't he? After all, *I* did.

She turns on him angrily

Paula Then you must have been spying on me!
Frank (*casually*) Yes. As a matter of fact I have.

Paula holds his look, then breaks away, dismissing him disparagingly

Paula Somehow I didn't imagine you in a dirty raincoat and a bowler hat.

Act I, Scene 1

A pause. He looks at her innocently

How long have you been watching me?

Frank (*with a smile*) Oh, I'd have to consult my records to give you the details.

Paula moves to him with sudden suspicion

Paula I'm not sure I believe a word you're saying. I'm not sure you know anything about me at *all* . . .

He looks back at her steadily

Frank Whether *I* know isn't important, though, is it? It's whether *James* knows.

A pause. Then Paula breaks away nervously

Paula Where the hell is Mark?
Frank Well—don't you want to know?
Paula Know what?
Frank How I can help you.
Paula (*dismissively*) I don't want to know anything about you at all!
Frank Oh, I expect you'll change your mind. You see, Paula—it is all right if I call you Paula? After all, I have had three of your vodkas and seen you in your dressing-gown—I don't think James would be awfully pleased if he found out about you. In fact, he'd be very unhappy. And I wouldn't like my old friend to be unhappy.

She returns to him angrily

Paula If you don't get out of here I shall call the police!
Frank The police? Whatever will you tell them?
Paula (*nervously*) I'll—I'll tell them you broke into my house.
Frank But I didn't. (*Pointedly*) You opened the front door *yourself*. Don't you remember? (*He moves towards the desk*) Tell me, Paula—how would you feel about . . . divorce?
Paula What are you talking about?
Frank Well, it's probably what James will want. If he finds out about you and Mark—and all the others. (*He moves back towards her*) And with you being the guilty party—in duplicate, as it were—you wouldn't do awfully well financially, would you? And you're very fond of money, aren't you, Paula? Oh, don't look like that. It's no crime to be fond of money. But, of course, if you *are* so very fond of luxury you do have to be awfully careful about lovers.

A long pause. Paula moves away a little

Paula How much do you want?

Frank looks puzzled

Frank H'm?
Paula Isn't that what this is all about? Money—to stop you telling James.

He looks appalled

Frank I wouldn't dream of telling James. *I* don't want him to know any more than *you* do.

Paula (*puzzled*) Then—what have you come here for?

He smiles

Frank Well, you see, Paula—the trouble is, I worry. About my friends. (*He sighs*) Poor James. I worry about him a *lot*. About him finding out—things that would—hurt him. So, you see, I want to be sure—absolutely sure—that James isn't *going* to be hurt. Do you understand? I want to be sure he never finds out about you and Mark, and all the others. I want to be sure. And I'm *going* to be sure.

Paula is now beginning to get nervous and apprehensive

Paula I—I want you to go.

But Frank just wanders away thoughtfully towards the bookshelves

Frank How much do you *read*, Paula?
Paula Read? Why?
Frank *I* read. Magazines mainly. I read a lot of magazines. And that's what gave me the idea.
Paula Wh-what idea?
Frank For coming here tonight—to see you. It was a magazine I was reading. At the dentist's, as a matter of fact. It was very interesting. Do you know how many fatal accidents there are in this country every year?
Paula (*slightly bemused*) Thousands, I should think . . .
Frank That's exactly what it said in the magazine. And I found that very interesting. (*He chuckles*) But then it was my turn for the dentist and I had to leave the magazine behind. (*His smile fades*) But I went on *thinking* about it. And I began to wonder how many of those accidents—hadn't *really* been accidents at all.

She is very still for a moment

Paula (*quietly*) Please go—I want you to go.
Frank There's no need to be frightened.
Paula Look—Mark will be here any minute!
Frank (*moving slowly towards her*) Oh, I don't know about that.
Paula What do you mean?
Frank (*quietly*) Well, for all we know he may be walking. It might take him quite a long time. So you see, don't you, what it is that I have in mind?
Paula (*frightened*) I—I'm not sure . . .
Frank Well, accidents do happen, don't they? That's what I read at the dentist's. So—suppose—just suppose for the sake of argument—that there was an accident—*here*—then James would never have to know about you—and Mark and all the others.

Paula moves slowly towards the windows, wishing that Mark would come quickly

Act I, Scene 1

Paula You—you'd never get away with it.

Frank follows her slowly

Frank But it would be an accident.
Paula Somebody will have seen you arriving here.
Frank What difference does that make?
Paula They'd remember! Somebody would remember seeing you! If anything happened to *me*—the police would find out . . .
Frank (*puzzled*) To *you*? But why should anything happen to you?

She looks at him, bewildered

Paula Isn't that—what you meant?

He smiles broadly

Frank No, of course not! You didn't think that I was going to . . . ? (*He laughs*) Oh, dear. No, no—I don't want to harm *you*. I told you—I want to help you.
Paula Why? Why should you want to help *me*? You've only just met me.
Frank Yes. I know. But don't forget—I have been *watching* you . . .

A moment, then she breaks away nervously to the windows

Paula I'm sure I heard a taxi . . .
Frank (*forcefully*) If there "happened" to be an accident—and James was killed—you'd get everything, wouldn't you? You could have the luxury—*and* the lovers.

Paula turns and looks at him in horror

Paula *James?* You—you can't really mean that!
Frank Why not? I've been thinking about it for months.
Paula Thinking about—killing James?

He shrugs and moves away towards the desk

Frank I'd rather call it protecting James.
Paula But you said you didn't want him hurt! You wanted to be sure he wasn't going to be hurt!
Frank Exactly. This way I'll be protecting him from the truth. If James knew the truth about you, he wouldn't *want* to live. So, don't you see, in a way I'd be doing him a favour.

Paula moves slowly towards him in horror

Paula You're not—not really—seriously suggesting . . . ?
Frank (*lightly*) Why not? I think I'd be quite good at arranging an accident.

A pause. Then the doorbell rings. Paula looks relieved

Paula Mark! (*She rushes to the door and opens it*)

Mark stands there, a little dishevelled and breathless. He is about twenty-five, good-looking and obviously attractive. He comes in, carrying a bunch of flowers

Paula closes the door and embraces him thankfully. He does not see Frank

Where the hell have you *been*?
Mark I couldn't get a taxi for ages. I'm awfully sorry.
Frank (*jovially*) I understand your car broke down.

Mark turns, sees Frank and is embarrassed

Mark Oh—sorry—I didn't know anyone was . . . (*He peters out, then in explanation of their embrace*) We're old friends.
Frank Yes. I know.
Paula This is Mark.

Mark comes into the room to meet Frank. Paula follows behind him

Frank (*smiling*) Is it really? You know, I thought it might be. (*To Mark*) I'm Frank. I bet you didn't know that.
Mark How do you do.

Mark almost drops the flowers, in his attempt to shake hands

Frank Ah! you shouldn't have brought me flowers.

Mark hands the flowers awkwardly to Paula

Oh, they're for *you*! I *am* disappointed.
Mark A bit bedraggled, I'm afraid. I dropped them getting into the taxi.

Paula puts the flowers down on the sofa table

Frank (*to Mark*) I'd better pour you a drink. You look as if you could do with one.

Mark looks surprised at Frank being so much at home here

Paula (*coldly*) You needn't bother. I can manage.

She goes to pour Mark a drink. Frank peers at Mark with a smile. Mark shifts uncomfortably

Frank We thought you were never going to get here.
Mark I'm—I'm a friend of James.
Frank Yes. I know. So am I. Perhaps we should form a club. We could have a tie with a photo of James rampant in the middle.

Mark looks a little alarmed

Mark He's not here, is he?
Frank Oh, no. You needn't worry. (*He smiles reassuringly*)
Mark What?
Frank He's out at a meeting. Isn't he, Paula?

Mark notices the use of the Christian name. Paula gives Frank a look and goes to Mark with his drink

Paula Here you are.
Mark (*taking it*) Thanks.

Act I, Scene 1

Frank smiles hospitably at Mark

Frank There! That'll make you feel better. What time have you booked the table for?

Mark (*uncertainly*) W-what?

Frank turns to Paula

Frank You did say you were going out to dinner didn't you, Paula?

Paula It's all right, Mark. I told him.

Mark Oh—er—not till eight-thirty. (*Nervously*) Cheers!

Frank Cheers! I won't have another, thank you, Paula. (*To Mark*) I've had three already. That's one thing you can say about Paula and James. They're very generous with their drinks.

Mark looks at Paula

Paula Frank called in unexpectedly. To see James. He was just going, as a matter of fact, when you arrived. (*Pointedly*) Weren't you, Frank?

Frank H'm? (*Taking the hint*) Ah—yes—yes, of course! I must be off. (*To Mark*) I only stayed to keep Paula company until you turned up.

Mark (*without enthusiasm*) That was very good of you.

Frank Not at all. My pleasure. Actually, I was just saying to Paula that if you didn't turn up soon *I'd* have to take her out to dinner. (*He chuckles*)

This does not please Mark too much; or Paula, for that matter

So it's a good thing you arrived or you might have lost her.

Paula (*with an edge*) I'll tell James you called.

Frank looks at her steadily

Frank That's up to you, isn't it? (*A brief pause—then he prepares to leave*) Well—I expect I'll be seeing you. Nice to have met you, Mark. Thanks for the drink, Paula. I—I'll give you a ring about that other matter.

Frank smiles and goes, closing the door behind him

A pause. Paula is edgy and thoughtful

Mark He's—he's very friendly.

Paula Yes ...

Mark You must have known him a long time.

Paula No. No, I haven't. I—I hardly know him at all. He's an old friend of James. They used to work together at one time. (*She goes to get her handbag from the armchair*)

Mark Oh, I see. And what does he do now?

Paula I don't know.

Mark (*with a smile*) An old friend of James and you don't know what he does for a living?

Paula I think he's a sales rep. or something.

A pause. Paula gets ready to leave

Mark I'm surprised he never mentioned it.

Paula Sorry?
Mark Frank. What he does for a living.
Paula I told you. I don't know him very well.
Mark (*with a grin*) That wasn't the impression *I* got!
Paula (*irritably*) Oh, for heaven's sake, what does it matter? He came to see James. James wasn't in. I gave him a drink. That's all there is to it.

A brief pause

Mark *Three* drinks.
Paula What?
Mark He said you gave him three drinks.
Paula For God's sake, stop being so bloody suspicious! There's nothing going on between us, if that's what you think!
Mark Paula . . .
Paula Look—I'm not in the mood for a lot of questions. All right?

Mark is surprised to find himself under attack

Mark I'm sorry. I didn't mean to . . .
Paula (*abruptly*) Oh, never mind! (*She goes to pour herself another drink*)
Mark (*after a moment*) Haven't you had enough of that?
Paula If I have it's your fault for turning up late! (*She refills her glass*)

He watches her, troubled and concerned. She takes her drink and goes to sit in the armchair. He goes across to her and squats down beside her. She looks at him for a moment. Then she smiles, puts a hand out to touch him

(*Gently*) I'm sorry.
Mark (*quietly*) I love you, Paula.

She looks at him warmly

Paula Yes. I know you do—but you mustn't.

He shrugs

Mark Can't help it, can I?

She looks at him tenderly. Then they kiss and both enjoy it. Finally she breaks away, rises and wanders off restlessly. He watches her go, puzzled by her mood

What's the matter? Is something wrong?
Paula (*evasively*) No. Why?
Mark There *is* something. I can tell. What are you thinking about?
Paula It's nothing, really! I expect I'm a bit tired. Frank was here rather a long time.

Mark looks down. They are back on Frank again

Mark I can't think why he bothered to call in anyway.
Paula Why?
Mark When he knew James was at a meeting.

Act I, Scene 1   17

Paula (*patiently*) He didn't know that when he arrived, did he? Not until I told him.
Mark Surprising he didn't check with James first, though, isn't it? Them being such old friends. Only had to lift the telephone.

She says nothing. He watches her for a moment. Much as he wants to, he cannot drop the subject

What had he been talking to you about?
Paula (*wearily*) Mark—I can't remember. General conversation. Nothing important. Does it matter?
Mark Well, he obviously upset you.
Paula He didn't upset me.
Mark Well, if he didn't, you seem to be in a funny sort of mood.
Paula I'm perfectly all right!
Mark If you're worried about something—if something's making you unhappy—tell me. Perhaps I can help.
Paula Mark, darling—I'm not unhappy. I'm not worried. I'm just a little bit tired. Come on—let's go and have dinner. (*With a smile*) I expect I'm hungry.

He kisses her, lightly at first, then more seriously. As they are kissing there is the sound of a key in the lock of the front door. They look towards the door, alarmed

(*In a whisper*) James!
Mark (*in a whisper*) It can't be! You said he was going to be late tonight.

They break apart

The door opens and James walks in. He is a good-looking man in his late forties. He is smartly dressed and carries a brief-case and an evening paper. He sees Paula and looks surprised

James Hullo, darling!
Paula James! You said you were going to be late.
James Yes, I know. And *you* said you were going *out*.
Paula Well, I am, but . . .
James You'd better hurry, then. It's after eight. (*He kisses Paula briefly and then sees Mark with apparent surprise*) Oh, hullo, Mark. How are you?
Mark (*nervously*) Er—fine, thanks.

James goes to shake hands with Mark

James (*jovially*) Good. Good. Paula's going out to dinner with an old schoolfriend. Did she tell you? They're going to have too much to drink and giggle over memories of dorm feasts and gym-slips.
Mark Really?
James How nice of you to call in, Mark. I was thinking it was time we met up again.
Mark Yes. I—I thought I'd pop in—on the off-chance of catching you.

James Splendid! (*He goes to put down his briefcase and newspaper on the desk*) I was going to ring you about a spot of lunch next week. But now you're here how about a television supper? There's bound to be something cold in the fridge.

Mark glances quickly at Paula

Mark Well—as a matter of fact, I . . .
Paula (*a little too abruptly*) I was stood up, James!
James I beg your pardon?
Paula Gillian rang and said she couldn't make dinner tonight after all. Her aunt turned up unexpectedly.
James Not the one from Stoke Poges?
Paula Yes.
James (*to Mark*) Fancy turning up unexpectedly from Stoke Poges. Good heavens! *My* only aunt lives in the Hebrides, so there's not much chance of *her* popping in. Now—everyone got a drink?
Mark I won't have another, thank you, James.
James Ah. You've had one already. Good. Good. (*To Paula*) You got one, darling?
Paula Yes, thank you.
James Right. Just me, then.

James goes to pour himself a whisky. Paula and Mark exchange a look. Paula goes to James, tentatively

Paula James, I—I booked a table at the restaurant.

James is busy with his drink

James H'm?
Paula For me and Gillian.
James I should jolly well hope so. They always get very booked on a Friday evening.
Paula It seems a pity to cancel it.
James Bit late to cancel it, anyhow. Why don't you take Mark? He looks as if he could do with a square meal.
Mark (*nervously*) Well—er—don't *you* want to go?

James returns with his drink

James No, no. I'm rather tired, as a matter of fact. I'll be much better off with cold meat, a glass of wine and the highlights of the cricket. (*He sits wearily in the armchair with his drink*)
Paula Are you sure, darling?
James Positive. You two run along and have a nice time.
Mark Well—if you're sure you don't mind . . .
James I insist. Anyway, you're all dressed up. You don't want to go back to your flat for fish fingers, do you? And Paula's got her new dress on, so you'll make a very attractive couple.

Paula and Mark exchange a quick glance, not sure if James is suspicious or not

Paula There's some chicken in the fridge and ...
James No, no. I tell you what. I'll make myself a Spanish omelette. (*To Mark*) I'm rather good at Spanish omelettes, you know. Ever since we took a villa on the Costa Brava a couple of years ago. What time did you book for?
Paula } Eight-thirty. } (*Speaking together*)
Mark

They both stop, but too late. James gives a tiny, secret smile and glances at his watch

James You'd better get a move on, then.
Mark Yes. I'll—I'll go and get a taxi.
James Good idea.

Mark starts to go

Maybe see you later.

Mark stops

Pop in for a nightcap when you get back, if you feel like it.
Mark Oh. Right. Thanks.
Paula (*to James*) Knowing you, you'll be fast asleep.
James Why? You're not going to be as late as all that, are you?

A moment

Mark I'll get the taxi.
James Good-bye, Mark!

Mark goes quickly

James turns to look at Paula with a secret smile

He's a nice boy, isn't he? Always so helpful.
Paula Are you *sure* you don't mind?
James H'm?
Paula My going out to dinner with him.
James Of course not, darling. I've got some things to see to, anyway. (*He goes to get the evening paper from the desk*) You go and have a nice time. Enjoy yourself.
Paula You sound almost glad to get rid of me.
James I thought I was being rather tolerant and understanding. (*He moves with the newspaper to the sofa*)
Paula We can easily cancel the table ...
James Don't keep on about it, darling. It's nice for you to go out with other men occasionally.

Paula prepares to go and picks up her stole. James notices something on the sofa table

Paula ...

Paula stops and looks at him

Paula Yes?

James Has—has somebody *else* been here tonight?

A pause. Paula is still

Paula Er—no. No—I don't think so. Why?

James holds up the end of a cigar he has found in the ashtray

James Well, *I* don't smoke cigars.

A pause

Paula Oh—that was probably Mark. I think *he* had one.
James I didn't think Mark smoked them, either.
Paula Well, he *must* have done, mustn't he?

James picks up Frank's empty glass from the sofa table

James There's another glass here as well. Don't tell me that Mark had one drink out of two glasses?

A pause, then Paula pretends to remember

Paula Oh—of course! How silly of me. I forgot. It was Frank.

James turns to look at her

James Frank?
Paula Yes. He—he popped in on the off-chance of seeing you.
James How very popular I am tonight! Everybody popping in to see me. (*Enthusiastically*) So you've met Frank at last, then? Good!
Paula Yes.

James sits on the sofa with his paper

James (*gently*) I can't think why you didn't say so in the first place instead of denying it like that.
Paula Denying what?
James That Frank had been here. Smoking cigars and drinking my drink.
Paula (*smiling nervously*) You don't begrudge him a drink, surely?
James I didn't say I begrudged him it, darling. I just didn't know why you should deny it.
Paula (*edgily*) I didn't deny it. I'd just forgotten, that's all. Why? It doesn't matter, does it?
James I didn't say it mattered, darling. (*He continues to read his newspaper*) Well, you'd better hurry up. Mark will be waiting with the meter ticking over.
Paula Yes. All right. (*She puts on a cosy smile and kisses him lightly*), Bye, darling. See you later.
James Yes.

Paula opens the front door

Have a nice time.

Paula looks at him for a moment, then smiles

Act I, Scene 2   21

Paula Yes. Thanks.

Paula goes out, closing the door behind her

James is absolutely still for a moment, his eyes in his newspaper; then he gets up, puts the paper down and goes across to look out of the window, watching them drive off. He looks at his watch. The telephone rings. He looks at it, hesitates for a moment, letting it ring. Then he goes and lifts the receiver

James Yes? ... Ah—hullo, Frank ... No ... No, there's nobody here now. Paula's gone out. I'm all on my own ... Right. I'll expect you in half an hour, then.

James hangs up, thoughtfully, and looks slowly towards the front door, as the Lights fade to a Black-out, and—

the CURTAIN *falls*

SCENE 2

The same. Early evening the following day

It is warm and pleasant. The doors to the garden are open

The telephone is ringing. After a moment Paula comes in from the bedrooms. She looks at the telephone, slightly apprehensive, then goes and lifts the receiver

Paula Hullo? ... (*She is not pleased*) What do *you* want? ... Yes—yes, I know all that but—look, there's nothing to discuss!

James comes in from the garden, carrying his briefcase. She does not see or hear him

(*Firmly*) Yes, I *do* mean it so please don't ring again. (*She hangs up abruptly, turns and finds James there. She jumps with fright*) Oh!
James Sorry, darling.
Paula You gave me such a fright—I didn't know you were there.
James Was that for me? (*He goes to the desk with his briefcase*)
Paula Oh—no. No. Wrong number. (*She pulls herself together*) You must have been up bright and early this morning. I haven't seen you all day.
James Had a few things to see to.
Paula Your car was still outside so I didn't think you could have gone very far.
James Derek picked me up. We had lunch at the Club.

The telephone rings again. A moment's indecision, then Paula goes for it, but James is nearer and picks up the receiver first

Hullo? Hullo—who *is* that? ... (*Whoever it is hangs up*) Must have got the wrong number again. (*He replaces the receiver*)

Paula moves to him

Paula I'm sorry about last night.

He looks puzzled

James Last night?
Paula I was a bit sharp with you.
James I'm the one who should apologize. I was in bed. Fast asleep when *you* came in. (*He starts to sort out some papers from his briefcase*)
Paula (*moving away*) I wasn't all *that* late.
James Oh, well, I expect I was early. (*Suddenly*) Good Lord!
Paula What's the matter.
James I completely forgot. I asked Mark back for a nightcap. How very rude of me not to stay up.
Paula Oh, he—he didn't come back here.
James He didn't?
Paula No. We each got a taxi from the restaurant.
James How very extravagant! Good meal, was it?
Paula Wonderful.
James Splendid. (*Pause*) Oh, by the way—you're not going out *tonight*, are you?
Paula Tonight? No. Why?
James I just wondered. You haven't got any—*plans* for tonight, then?
Paula (*puzzled*) Plans? No.
James Oh, good. Good.
Paula Why? Is something special happening tonight?
James (*airily*) Oh, no. I just wanted you to be in, that's all.
Paula (*with a smile*) All right. Then I *will* be. We can have a quiet dinner. Just the two of us.
James Good.

James puts some of the papers back into his briefcase. Paula starts to go

(*Casually*) How did you get on with Frank?

Paula stops

Paula H'm?
James Last night. It must have been quite a surprise for you, him turning up on the doorstep like that.
Paula Yes. I'd no idea who he was.
James (*moving in a little*) I'm sorry about that. I've been meaning to have him over for dinner so you could both meet. Just didn't seem to get around to it. Still—you've met now, anyhow. That's the main thing.
Paula Yes.
James He's a nice chap. I'm very fond of him. (*He starts to go back to the desk*)
Paula How long has he been back from Australia?

James stops and looks at her

James Oh, he told you about Australia, then?
Paula Yes. How long has he been back?

Act I, Scene 2

James (*vaguely*) Oh, I dunno. Two or three months, I suppose. He—he takes a bit of getting to know. Not much of a conversationalist, old Frank.
Paula He talked a lot last night.
James Did he? Good Lord. (*He puts his briefcase away*) What about?

Paula drifts towards the sofa table to get herself a cigarette

Paula (*vaguely*) Oh—the house, the weather—you know.

He moves towards her a little with a folder containing some papers

James Was he here very long?
Paula No. Not really.
James Did he—talk a *lot* about Australia?
Paula Yes. He was very interesting.
James Good old Frank! He's usually quite shy with strangers. I'm surprised he stayed when he found I wasn't here. (*He glances idly at the documents in the folder*) Funny, y'know—I thought I'd *told* Frank I had a meeting last night. I'm surprised he expected me to be here. (*A pause. Casually*) Oh, by the way, Gillian rang last night.
Paula Gillian?
James Yes. She seemed to have forgotten all about your dinner date.

Paula hesitates for a second, then tries to cover

Paula Don't be silly, darling. She rang me last night to put it off. Don't you remember?
James Yes—I thought that was what you *said*. Still, you had a nice time. That's the main thing, isn't it? (*He sits in the armchair with the documents he is browsing through*)

Paula watches him for a moment in silence

Paula James . . .
James H'm?
Paula Why did Frank come back here last night?

He looks up, puzzled

James I don't understand.
Paula After Mark and I went out—Frank came *back* here, didn't he?

A silence

James Back *here*?
Paula Yes.

James looks puzzled

James What are you talking about? I was alone all the evening. I made my Spanish omelette, had a glass of wine, watched the telly for a bit and then went to bed. I certainly didn't have a visitor.

But Paula persists

Paula James—when I got back from the restaurant, I saw a man leaving this house.
James Leaving *here*?
Paula Yes. And I think he saw me because he turned quickly and went off in the opposite direction. I could have sworn it was Frank.
James Well, I can't think what he was doing out there. And if it *was* Frank why should he run away when he saw you?
Paula You're quite *sure* he didn't visit you after Mark and I had gone?
James (*with a smile*) Of course I'm sure. I think I'd have remembered. You must have been mistaken. After all, you only met him last night.
Paula I'm certain it was him ...
James (*lightly*) Well, I promise you, he wasn't here. And Frank's hardly likely to come all this way just to wander around the garden, is he? (*He chuckles*) He'd certainly have popped in for a chat. Especially as he knew I was on my own. Darling, it was dark and you made a mistake.
Paula (*unconvinced*) Yes. Yes, I suppose I must have done ...

He looks at her thoughtfully

James Anyway, it's—not very important, is it?

She decides to evade the issue

Paula No. No, of course not. (*She turns away*) I'd better see to the dinner. (*She starts to go*)

He watches her

James Darling ...
Paula (*stopping*) What?
James Is everything all right?

A brief pause

Paula Yes. Why?
James You seem a bit—on edge today.
Paula No. I'm all right. Really.

Paula goes quickly

James looks after her, thoughtfully, for a moment; then goes and closes the door. He crosses briskly to the telephone and dials a number. He looks towards the door to the kitchen while the number is ringing, to make sure she is not returning

James (*on the telephone, quietly*) Hullo? Frank? ... It's me—James. Look—I've been thinking about what you said last night. Why don't you come over here this evening? ... Yes ... Why not? The sooner the better. Then we can get everything over and done with ... All right. See you at about—oh—seven-thirty? ... Right. Good-bye. (*He hangs up*)

Paula enters quickly

Paula By the way, James ...!
James What's the matter?

Act I, Scene 2   25

Paula Did you remember my car?

James looks at her blankly for a moment

James Car?
Paula Yes. It was in for service. You said you'd collect it today.
James Oh, I'm so sorry. I'm afraid I forgot all about it. Never mind. We can pick it up on Monday.
Paula But I need it tomorrow morning.
James (*reasonably*) Surely we can manage with one car until Monday?
Paula No. I must have it today. (*Rather tartly*) I suppose that means I'll have to go and fetch it myself.
James Don't be silly, darling. You've got the dinner to see to.
Paula The dinner will just have to wait!
James No, no, Paula! It's out of the question. You've got far too much to do. (*He acts the long-suffering husband*) Don't worry—*I'll* go. If it's so important to you.
Paula But you've only just got back.
James (*with a smile*) Well, presumably that won't have to matter, will it? Anyway, perhaps the walk will do me good.
Paula It's not very far. (*Lightly*) And it *was* you who forgot it the first time.
James (*smiling tolerantly*) All right—I'm on my way.
Paula Thank you, darling. George said he'd leave the keys in the boot where he always does.
James Okay. I'll find them. (*He starts to go towards the windows*) But I really don't see why it can't wait until Monday.

James goes out through the windows and disappears down the garden

Paula goes to the windows and watches him go, thoughtfully. Then she looks at her wristwatch, puts out her cigarette and empties the ashtray into the wastepaper basket near the desk

She glances around the room and, apparently satisfied, goes out to the kitchen. There is quite a long silence. Then the doorbell rings: loudly. Paula returns a little puzzled, and goes to open the front door. Mark stands there

Paula is not pleased

Paula What the hell are *you* doing here?
Mark Paula—there are things we've got to talk about!

Paula comes down the steps into the sitting-room angrily

Paula I told you not to come here.

He closes the front door and follows her, reassuringly

Mark All right. All right. Don't panic. I saw James going off down the road, so I knew the coast was clear.
Paula Well, he won't be very long. (*She turns to him*) Look—I told you last night—we've got to stop seeing each other.
Mark Yes, I know that's what you *said*, but . . .

Paula For the time being, that's all!
Mark Well, I've been awake all night thinking about it. And I simply don't understand you. How can we stop seeing each other—just like that? I *need* you, Paula!
Paula (*reasonably*) Look—I think James is suspicious. And *I* don't want him to find out. All right?
Mark Why not?
Paula (*wearily*) Oh, Mark, for heaven's sake . . .! (*She breaks away from him*)
Mark *I* don't mind! I want you to leave James. You know that.
Paula Don't be silly. It wouldn't work.
Mark Why not? I love you.
Paula So does James.
Mark (*angrily*) And if you left him you'd leave all *this*, as well! Is that it?

She does not reply. He moves away like a caged lion

You've really got it made, haven't you? You've got *either* of us! *Both* of us!
Paula (*coldly*) If you don't like the arrangement, Mark, you don't have to put up with it.
Mark (*returning to her quickly*) I'm sorry—I didn't mean to say that. It's just that—that I don't know what I'm going to do without you.
Paula (*thoughtfully*) Well—it may not be for very long.

A pause. He looks at her, puzzled

Mark What do you mean?
Paula (*evasively*) I mean you've just got to be patient, that's all. (*She turns away*)
Mark (*going to her*) No, wait a minute. You said, "It may not be for very long". What does that mean? Have you thought of a way out of it?

Paula escapes from him and goes nervously towards the windows

Paula No—no, of course not. But—well—we don't know how things are going to work out, do we? Ever.

He follows her

Mark (*with a glimmer of hope*) You mean—you might decide to leave James?
Paula No, Mark. I told you. I'm not leaving James. (*She sees his desperately sad face*) Oh, darling, don't look like that . . .
Mark You don't really love me a bit, do you?
Paula Of course I do.
Mark But you're staying with James.
Paula Yes.
Mark (*vehemently*) I won't *let* you!
Paula (*gently*) Don't be silly, darling . . .
Mark I mean it! I love you too much. I'm not going to just call it off—postpone it indefinitely until the coast is clear—I'm going to *tell* James!

I'm going to wait here until he comes back and I'm going to tell him! I'm going to tell him *tonight*!
Paula (*calmly but firmly*) No, Mark.
Mark (*defiantly*) You can't stop me.
Paula No, I can't! But it wouldn't do any good.
Mark We'll see about that!
Paula No, Mark—please! You mustn't tell James!

He holds her look for a moment, then breaks away from her. She goes to him and speaks gently

We've just got to be patient.
Mark (*turning*) We?
Paula Don't you think it affects me, too? But *I* know we've got to be sensible. In a little while—maybe it'll be all right again.

A moment, then he kisses her impulsively. This time she shows more enthusiasm, but whether just for his sake is hard to tell. They break

You must go now. He'll be back soon.

He nods, trying to be sensible

Mark All right. All right. Good-bye, darling. Telephone me?

She nods

Paula Promise. Go now.

Mark smiles, kisses her again quickly, goes out through the windows and disappears down the garden

Paula watches him go, thoughtfully

Susan comes in from the bedrooms

Susan Hullo, Paula . . .

Susan is James's daughter. A pleasant, intelligent, charming girl of nineteen. She is vivacious, but not beautiful like her stepmother. Paula turns and sees her

Paula Susan! How long have *you* been there?
Susan (*with a shrug*) Not very long . . . (*But obviously long enough to have heard something*)
Paula (*with a smile that could slice bacon*) Don't they teach you at college that it's rude to listen to other people's conversations?
Susan Sorry, I didn't realize it was private. I'm a bit disorientated. I'm afraid. Whatever time is it?
Paula (*looking at her watch*) Six o'clock.
Susan Good heavens, I must have been asleep for ages!
Paula Why? What time did you get here?
Susan Oh, it must have been about three, I suppose. You and Daddy were out so I thought I'd have a lie down. I was up a bit late last night. We had a party. I must have gone right off.

Paula tries to appear unconcerned

Paula Well, this certainly *is* a surprise! I *didn't* know you were coming this week-end, did I?

Susan looks a little shamefaced

Susan Er—no. I'm afraid not.
Paula Oh, that's all right, then. I thought perhaps I'd forgotten.
Susan It was a last-minute decision. I wanted to surprise you.
Paula Well, you certainly did that!

Susan moves away

Susan Yes. I'm sorry. (*Pause*) I didn't mean to listen into your conversation.
Paula That's all right. It's just that I'm not a great one for surprises.
Susan I'm sorry. (*Pause*) Who is he?
Paula H'm? Oh—Mark! (*Lightly*) He's just a silly boy who thinks he's fallen in love with me. A friend of your father's, too! Isn't that embarrassing? And he simply won't take no for an answer. I can't think what I'm going to do about him.
Susan (*a little icily*) You seemed to be doing all right.

Paula goes to Susan, thinking it best to try to be friendly

Paula You see, Susan—the trouble is that the way he was talking just now he really *might* go and tell James. And James might actually believe that there's something in it.
Susan And there isn't?
Paula Of course there isn't! But James does tend to be a bit jealous and he might believe him. (*Trying to be cosy*) So, for heaven's sake, don't tell him what you heard, will you? Let it be our little secret.
Susan (*coolly*) Don't worry, Paula. I wasn't going to tell Daddy. (*Pause*) Have you known him very long?
Paula A few months. James invited him to dinner one evening.
Susan Do you see him very often?
Paula He's a friend of James, so naturally we see him occasionally.
Susan That isn't what I meant.

A pause. Paula considers how to handle the situation

Paula You know, you really mustn't jump to conclusions. Look, I—I don't mean this unkindly, but I imagine you know rather more about the piano than you do about men. If I hadn't given Mark a little *hope*—well, he might have exaggerated everything to James. And that might have hurt your father. And you wouldn't want that, would you?
Susan (*levelly*) I'm sure you know what you're doing, Paula.

A moment

James comes in from the garden dragging a rather furtive-looking Mark

James I say, Paula! Look what *I've* found!

Paula looks far from pleased

Act I, Scene 2   29

You should have seen him! He was wandering down the road in a dream so I dragged him in. (*To Mark*) You weren't going to disappear without calling on us, were you, Mark?

James sees Susan for the first time. He looks surprised, and for some reason not entirely pleased

Sue . . .
Susan Hullo, Daddy! (*She waits for his enthusiasm*) Well? Aren't you pleased to see me?

James pulls himself together and goes to Susan enthusiastically

James Oh, yes! Yes—of course—of course I am! Delighted. I just didn't know you were coming home this week-end.
Susan I know. That was the idea. I wanted to surprise you all. I'm very sorry.
James Don't be silly. I'm glad to see you. We *all* are. It's a wonderful surprise! (*They embrace*) But you should have telephoned.

James and Susan laugh, enjoying each other's company

Susan It wouldn't have been a surprise, then, would it? (*Suspiciously*) You haven't got something special on tonight, have you?

A brief pause

James No. No, of course not. Come and say hullo. (*He hands her across to Mark*) This is Mark. Mark, this is Susan. Mark's one of our dearest friends. Right, Paula?

Paula makes no comment

Susan How do you do.
Mark How do you do.

They shake hands

Your father's told me all about you. I hear you play the piano beautifully.

Paula cuts across the conversation

Paula James, you got back very quickly. You did collect my car this time, didn't you?

James hangs his head guiltily

James Ah. No. No, I'm afraid I didn't.
Paula What!
James (*reasonably*) Well, they hadn't left the keys, darling.
Paula (*vehemently*) George always leaves them!

James tries to be patient

James Well, he hadn't left them this time.
Paula Are you sure you looked properly?

James looks at Susan with a grin and raises his eyes to heaven

James Yes, darling. Quite sure.
Paula Oh, God . . .!
James (*to Mark, with a smile*) There's always a drama when Paula's car's being serviced.
Susan It's a pity I *didn't* tell you I was coming for the week-end, then. *I* could have done it.

Mark looks at her in surprised admiration

Mark Good Lord! Don't tell me you know all about *cars* as well as pianos?
Susan It's cheaper to do it yourself.
James But you haven't got a car.
Susan I have now.
Paula (*coldly*) You're full of surprises today, aren't you?
Susan It's only a little banger. Wasn't very expensive. But I've been learning what to do when it breaks down.
Paula (*still grumbling*) I just don't understand it. George has never forgotten the keys before.
James Well, it's hardly the end of the world, darling. We can collect the car on Monday.
Paula But I need it first thing tomorrow morning.

James is getting a little embarrassed by her over-reaction to the matter of the car

James Look—there's no problem. You can borrow mine. (*He turns to Mark to change the subject*) Mark, I've got a wonderful idea. Why don't you come to dinner tonight?

Paula looks far from pleased. Mark looks at her uncertainly

Mark Er—well, I . . .
James Now that Sue's here—let's make it a party.

Mark and Susan look at each other

Paula (*aside to James*) What are you up to?

James looks directly at her

James (*quietly*) I'm not up to anything, Paula. (*He turns to Mark again*) Well, Mark? What do you say?
Mark Well, I . . .
Paula Darling, you mustn't bully people. Mark has probably got other plans for tonight.
James Oh? *Have* you, Mark?
Mark (*taking the hint*) Well—er—yes, as a matter of fact, I—I was thinking of going to the pictures.
James You can go to the pictures anytime. Besides, I owe you a dinner after last night.
Susan Oh? What happened last night?

James Mark stepped into the breech when Paula was stood up by an old schoolfriend. He took her out to dinner. It was very kind of him and I appreciate it.
Susan (*with a smile*) Presumably Paula was quite pleased as well.

Paula flashes her a look

James Good! That's settled, then.

Embarrassed, Paula speaks quietly to James

Paula Darling, I—I hadn't exactly catered for a dinner party. You said it was just going to be the two of us.
James Good heavens, you've got a chicken casserole out there that's big enough to feed an army. It's all settled, and I'm going to freshen up a bit. (*He starts to go*) Make yourself at home, Mark. (*He grins at Paula*) Well, we're going to have quite a party, after all, aren't we, Paula? Five of us. (*He makes for the door*)

Paula looks puzzled

Paula Five?

James pauses in the doorway

James Oh, didn't I tell you? I've asked Frank over for dinner.

James goes

A moment. Paula is still. Mark looks at her. Susan notices the look, then moves towards Paula

Susan Who's Frank?
Paula Oh, he—he used to work with James a long time ago. When you were a little girl. Frank Henderson.
Susan (*remembering*) Oh. Oh, yes, of course! I remember. But I thought he went to live abroad. Australia or somewhere?
Paula Yes. He's back now. Been back about six months, apparently ... (*She throws a look towards the door*) But I wish your father hadn't asked him to dinner *tonight*.

Mark notices her strong reaction, and then breaks the atmosphere

Mark Well, I'd better go home and change.
Susan Don't be silly. You're perfectly all right like that. Isn't he, Paula?
Paula (*miles away*) Yes. Yes, of course.
Mark Oh, no! I know James. He's very formal about dinner parties. Anyhow, I can't sit here until eight o'clock. Besides, I want to make a good impression on your daughter. (*He grins at Susan*)
Susan Oh—well, if *you're* going to dress up I suppose *I* shall have to.
Mark (*smiling*) I should jolly well hope so! You're not having dinner dressed like that.

They laugh. Susan goes towards the front door

Susan I'll just get my things out of the car.

Susan goes, leaving the door slightly ajar

Paula and Mark look at each other. He smiles sheepishly

Paula Couldn't you have kept out of sight?
Mark I didn't see him coming up the road.
Paula (*edgily*) Well, you could have made some excuse. You didn't have to say yes to dinner.
Mark It might have looked suspicious if I'd refused. (*He smiles*) Anyway, I *wanted* to come.

Paula gives him a weary look

James *asked* me! Surely he wouldn't have asked me to dinner if he thought I'd been having it off with his wife?
Paula He might.
Mark Oh, come on! I'm sure he's got no idea.
Paula Well, Susan has.

He looks at her in surprise

Mark What?
Paula Oh, yes. She knows all right.
Mark Don't be ridiculous!
Paula (*going to him*) She overheard part of our conversation. She was out there. Listening.
Mark How long?
Paula Long enough to know what's going on.
Mark Oh, Christ!
Paula (*urgently*) Look—you'll have to change your mind. You don't have to come back. You can easily ring up and say you've changed your mind.
Mark I can't do that. Not now. Anyhow, I thought perhaps you'd *want* me to be here.
Paula What do you mean?

He looks at her quizzically

Mark You didn't seem very happy about—Frank coming to dinner.
Paula It—it was just that James had asked him and hadn't told me anything about it.
Mark (*thoughtfully*) I wonder why.

A brief pause

Paula I—I expect he forgot. (*She thinks of something*) And yet ... (*She stops*)
Mark And yet what?
Paula Well, James and I talked about having dinner *alone* tonight, and he must have known then that Frank was coming ...
Mark And yet he never mentioned it?
Paula No.

Act I, Scene 2

Mark (*bemused*) I wish I knew what the hell is going on here tonight.

Paula looks at him

Paula So do I...

Susan enters, a bit breathless. She is carrying a plastic bag containing a dress and other items

Susan Right. There we are. Now I've got this lot, I'll try to make myself beautiful like you, Paula. (*She laughs at her own expense*)
Mark You look great as you are.
Susan Thank you very much. Liar!
Mark Well, I'm going to get a taxi. See you both later. Cheers!

Mark laughs and goes out into the garden. Paula has a sudden thought, collects her handbag on the way and follows him into the garden

Paula (*as she goes*) Oh—Mark! Just a minute! I've got an idea! Mark!

Susan watches her go, thoughtfully

James comes in. He stops, seeing Susan alone

James Oh. Where is everybody?
Susan In the garden. Mark's going to change.
James Change in the garden?

Susan laughs

Susan No—at home! And I'm going to put this on. (*She holds up the plastic bag that contains her dress*)
James Good heavens.
Susan I hope Paula didn't mind.
James What?
Susan My turning up unannounced. I don't want to upset her. That really would get the week-end off on the wrong foot, wouldn't it?
James (*gently remonstrating*) Now, now—that's enough of that.
Susan Well, I'm not exactly her favourite person, am I?
James Don't be silly. You mustn't imagine things.
Susan You know it's true. That's why I don't come home as often as I'd like.

He looks down, knowing it is the truth. He goes to her

James (*quietly*) Try to understand, darling. It's difficult for Paula. Not having children of her own. I suppose in a way she's—jealous.
Susan Of *me*? She's beautiful!
James That isn't everything, though, is it?

Paula enters from the garden

Susan starts to get her dress out of the bag

Paula Mark's gone home to change.
James Good heavens, he didn't need to do that.

Paula That's what I told him, but he insisted. And I thought he'd never get a taxi at this time so I . . .
Susan (*interrupting her*) Just look at those creases! (*She holds her dress out*) I'd better go and hang this up for a bit.
James I can't think why you don't pack your clothes properly.
Susan Don't panic. They'll soon hang out.

Susan grins at him and goes off to the bedrooms

Paula You didn't need to ask Mark to dinner, you know.

James turns to look at Paula

James Oh. I thought you'd be pleased.
Paula *I* had dinner with him last night.
James Never mind. He can talk to Susan and Frank.
Paula And why did you invite Frank? I don't understand. I thought you wanted to have a quiet evening. Just the two of us. That's what you said.
James Yes. Yes, I know, darling. (*He goes to pour himself a whisky*)
Paula Then why ask him?
James Well, I—er—I *didn't* exactly.
Paula What do you mean?
James He asked himself. Rang up and asked. I could hardly refuse.
Paula When?
James H'm?
Paula When did he ring up?
James Oh—when you were in the kitchen. I say, you lot must have been knocking back the vodka pretty fast last night. There's hardly any left. I'll have to send out for reinforcements.

James comes down with his whisky, chuckling. Paula moves to him

Paula (*persisting*) *Why* couldn't you refuse?
James Sorry?
Paula To invite Frank to dinner.
James Darling, does it matter?

Paula moves away

Paula I didn't particularly want him here tonight.
James Oh. Oh, I'm sorry. I didn't realize. (*With a slight edge*) After your long talk last night I thought perhaps you got on rather well.
Paula No. Not particularly.
James Well, this'll be a good chance for you to get to know each other, then, won't it?
Paula I really don't see why you . . . !
James (*firmly*) I didn't think you'd mind. Look—I feel sorry for Frank. After all, he hasn't been very successful and . . .

Paula turns sharply

Paula Perhaps that's *his* fault!
James I'm not so sure about that. And—in view of the past—I can't just

Act I, Scene 2

ignore him. It may be silly of me, but I feel in a way I'm responsible for him.
Paula Responsible!
James Look, you only met Frank for the first time last night. I can't understand how you can take such an instant dislike to him. For heaven's sake—give him a chance! (*He breaks away*)
Paula I just think you might have *told* me, that's all!

Paula stalks angrily out to the kitchen

James watches her go. He is thoughtful for a moment. He looks at his watch, glances briefly back towards the kitchen door and then goes to the windows. He takes the key out of the lock on the window and puts it in his pocket

Susan breezes in from the bedrooms

Susan It's worse than I thought. I'll have to press it.
James (*with a smile*) There you are. What did I tell you?
Susan You wouldn't know where the iron is, would you, Daddy?
James Yes, I would, as a matter of fact. In the cupboard next to the fridge.
Susan Oh, fine. (*She starts to go*)
James Don't suppose you feel like a walk, do you?

She stops and looks at him, a little surprised

Susan A walk?
James Well, it's a lovely evening.
Susan (*with a little laugh*) I thought we were getting ready for a dinner party.
James There's plenty of time. Besides, there isn't any vodka. Your mother and her boy-friends have scoffed the lot, so I'm off to the pub for reinforcements.
Susan What about my dress?
James You can do that when you come back.

She hesitates a moment

Susan No. No, I'd better help Paula with the dinner.
James There's nothing much to do. It's a casserole. Oh, come on. After all, I don't see you very often.

Susan is pleased and gives a little smile

Susan All right. You're on.
James Good!
Susan I'll just go and tell Paula.
James (*sharply*) No!

Susan stops and looks at him

You—you needn't bother.
Susan But hadn't we better tell her where we're going?
James (*lightly*) She'll guess. She knows we're short of vodka. Besides, we shan't be long.

Susan You don't think she'll mind? Being left all alone.

He laughs off the suggestion

James No, of course not! Don't be silly, darling. Why should she mind? Anyhow, we'll be back in no time. Come on!

James takes her arm and they go towards the windows

Susan All right, but if she's angry I shall blame it all on you!

Susan and James go off into the garden and disappear from sight, chattering happily. There is quite a pause, then Paula comes in from the kitchen, talking as she does so

Paula What time did you ask Frank to come, then? (*She stops, seeing nobody there. She looks around*) James . . . (*She looks puzzled, thinks for a moment and then goes to the door to the bedrooms. She looks inside and calls*) James . . .! (*Silence*) Susan! (*Silence*) James!! (*Silence She goes to the windows and looks out into the garden. She sees nobody. She steps outside and looks about. She calls out again*) James! Where are you? (*She comes back into the house, looking even more worried. She moves thoughtfully into the room*)

The telephone rings sharply. She jumps with fright

Oh! (*She goes to the telephone and lifts the receiver*) Hullo? (*Nobody speaks*) Hullo? Who is that? (*Nobody speaks*) Hullo?

She replaces the receiver, her fear and perplexity increasing. She decides to go for a drink and pours herself a whisky. Then she notices the open windows leading to the garden. She puts down the glass of whisky and crosses to the windows. She closes the windows, fastens the bolt on one of them and then goes to lock the other one. She discovers that the key is missing. She looks on the floor, thinking it must have dropped out. She cannot find it. She straightens up, thoughtful and nervous. She returns slowly to the drinks table and picks up her whisky. She takes a sip of it, anxiously. As she looks slowly and apprehensively back towards the windows, quiet ominous music creeps in and the Lights fade to Black-out

After a few moments the Lights fade up again on Scene 3

Scene 3

The same. An hour later

The Lights fade up on the empty room. The stereo is playing the Sibelius Second Symphony

A long pause: just the music playing. Then a man appears outside in the garden. He comes up to the windows and peers into the room. It is Frank. After a slight hesitation he opens the windows carefully and steps inside. He waits for a moment, listening, then closes the windows and fastens them. He hears a noise and stands very still above the windows, waiting

Act I, Scene 3

Paula comes in from the kitchen with a bowl of crisps and her half-empty glass. She does not see Frank. She puts the crisps down on the table above the sofa, almost finishes off her drink and goes to get a refill. At the last moment she sees Frank and screams, dropping her drink. She stays very still, breathing heavily, watching him as he moves towards her in silence

Frank (*finally*) I'm sorry. I didn't mean to frighten you.
Paula What the hell are you doing there?
Frank I'm coming to dinner.
Paula (*coldly*) People who come to dinner usually go to the front door. And they usually ring the bell.
Frank Oh, sorry. I thought—old friend of the family and all that . . .

Paula bends to pick up her glass

Here—let me do that. (*He goes to pick it up for her*)

She backs away from him nervously

What's the matter?
Paula Nothing . . .
Frank You look frightened.
Paula Well, you gave me a shock. I didn't know there was anyone here.

She moves away and turns off the stereo. He picks up the glass

Frank There we are. Nothing broken, anyway. That's something. Bit of a mess on the carpet, though. (*He rubs the carpet with his handkerchief*)
Paula It doesn't matter.
Frank Let me get you another drink.
Paula No, thank you.
Frank All right if I help myself then?
Paula Go ahead.
Frank Thanks. (*He goes to get himself a whisky*)

Paula wanders nervously across to the windows and looks out, hoping to see James. He turns with his drink and watches her for a moment

It was kind of James to invite me to dinner.
Paula (*turning*) Did he have any choice?

She moves away towards the sofa. He takes a sip of whisky, his eyes on her, then comes down to her

Frank Look—I'm sorry if I upset you. Coming in from the garden like that. I *should* have used the front door. It's just that last night when I did that I caught you in the bathroom. Didn't want to risk doing that again.
Paula I don't live alone. James could have answered the door.
Frank (*pointedly*) But James isn't here, though, is he?

Paula turns to look at him

Paula How do *you* know?

He smiles

Frank Well—unless he's hiding somewhere. (*He glances around the room*)

Paula is apprehensive and nervous. She moves away

Paula He won't be very long.
Frank Where did he go?

A pause

Paula I—I don't know.
Frank Didn't he tell you?
Paula Er—no. They must have gone for a walk.
Frank They?
Paula Yes. I—I think he's with Susan.
Frank Susan? Last night you never said she was coming to see you.
Paula I didn't know then. So they've probably gone for a walk.
Frank A bit late to go for a walk, isn't it? And without telling *you*?
Paula I don't expect they'll be very long.
Frank But you're not *sure* that he's with Susan?
Paula (*irritably*) Well, they've both disappeared so I assume they must be together!
Frank Yes. I suppose so. (*He puts his glass down on the armchair table and takes out a small cigar*) Well—it must be quite a weight off your mind.

Paula looks puzzled

Paula Sorry?
Frank Not to have to worry any more about what James might find out. You know—about you and Mark and all the others. (*He lights his cigar*)
Paula I'm sorry. I don't know what you're talking about.
Frank (*smiling*) Oh, come on. Don't look so gloomy. You should be pleased. After all, you didn't want to lose all this, did you? (*He indicates the room*) Now you don't *have* to lose it. Because James isn't going to know anything at all about you. Not *now*. (*He looks at her directly*)

Paula begins to have a fearful suspicion

Paula What are you trying to tell me? What have you done?

Frank just smiles. Paula crosses quickly to the windows and looks out into the garden. Then she turns abruptly to face him again

Frank! Is James all right?

Frank looks a little puzzled

(*Vehemently*) Where *is* he?!

Frank shrugs innocently

Frank *I* don't know. Any more than *you* do. (*He drifts away below the sofa, smoking his cigar*) You know, at first I didn't think you'd agree.
Paula Agree? To what?
Frank To my idea.

Watching him carefully, Paula crosses slowly towards him

Act I, Scene 3

Paula I never agreed to anything.

Frank turns to look at her

Frank Then you must have forgotten our conversation last night.
Paula (*carefully*) I remember every word of our conversation and I did not agree to anything.

Frank looks puzzled

Frank Not agree?
Paula To anything.
Frank I must have misunderstood. Are you *sure*?
Paula Quite sure.
Frank I thought we agreed that it would be to our mutual advantage if James had an accident.
Paula We never agreed to anything.

Frank looks disappointed

Frank Oh, dear. And I've been making plans . . .

A pause. Paula watches him carefully. Then she makes for the telephone and lifts the receiver

What are you going to do?
Paula I'm going to call the police and tell them what you threatened to do.

He shrugs

Frank All right. Go ahead.

She holds his look for a moment, then starts to dial

If you're prepared to take the consequences.

She stops dialling

Paula What do you mean?
Frank No, no—you go ahead. If that's what you want to do.

A pause

Paula What do you mean—take the consequences?
Frank Well—if you speak to the police—what will you tell them exactly? That I suggested that we murdered your husband?
Paula Yes.
Frank (*thoughtfully*) H'm. All right—go on.
Paula What?
Frank Tell them. Tell them that. But—they'll want to know why. You couldn't just tell them I'd suggested killing your husband for no reason. You'd have to tell them the reasons. You'd have to tell them about Mark. And—all the others. Dear me! All that dirty linen.

She replaces the receiver

Paula *You're* the one who suggested murder.

He smiles and sits on the sofa

Frank (*calmly*) Oh, I doubt if the police would believe that. They'd probably consider that my carefully collected information about you would be more use to me if James was alive. And anyhow if they *did* believe it they'd probably also believe that you were going to be an accessory.

She moves towards him

Paula (*desperately*) They'd believe me! And so would James! He'd believe me—and *forgive* me!
Frank Would he? Why didn't you tell him, then?

A brief pause

Paula What?
Frank Last night. Why didn't you tell him about our conversation last night? (*Pause*) You *didn't* tell him, did you?
Paula No . . .
Frank Why not? If you were so certain he'd believe you—and if you were so *against* the idea—why didn't you tell him what I was suggesting?

A pause. She looks away

Paula I—I don't know . . .

He smiles

Frank Perhaps because you weren't so much against the idea as you pretend.

She looks at him angrily for a moment

Paula Go to hell! (*She breaks away*)
Frank I know how you feel. At first *I* didn't think I could do it, either. Then, the more I thought about it—the easier the idea became.

Paula, her fears mounting, moves to him urgently

Paula Frank—I've got to know! Is—is James still *alive*?

A pause. He just looks at her

(*More vehemently*) Is he *alive*?

Frank smiles

Frank As far as I know. At the moment.

Paula faces him desperately

Paula Look—I'll give you seven thousand pounds. In cash. You can have it within three days. And then I want you to—to *please* go away and never—*ever*—come near me or my husband again.

She waits for his reaction. He says nothing

Well?

Act I, Scene 3   41

He smiles secretly and slowly shakes his head

Frank Sorry, Paula. That's no good at all.
Paula Why not?
Frank Because you took too long about it. And now it's too late.

She looks at him in horror

Paula What the hell do you mean?
Frank I told you. I've been making plans . . .

Paula gazes at him apprehensively

James and Susan come in from the garden, breathlessly. He is carrying a bottle of vodka

Paula breaks away from Frank, relieved to hear James's voice

James (*laughing*) Oh, dear! Oh, dear! I'm far too old for running up hills!
Susan I gave you twenty yards start.
James Not nearly enough!

James and Susan laugh

Paula James!

Paula goes quickly to James and clutches at him in relief

Where have you been? I didn't know where you were!
James Getting reinforcements. (*He waves the bottle of vodka*) Nothing to get excited about.
Paula But you've been gone for over an hour.
James Was it as long as that? Sorry, darling, but we got talking to a couple of the locals. You know how it is. They hadn't seen Sue for ages.
Paula Well, you might have told me where you were going. (*She turns away from him*)

James and Susan look at each other guiltily

Susan (*to James, quietly*) There! What did I tell you?

James looks across at Frank

James Ah—hullo, Frank! Sorry I wasn't here when you arrived. I hope Paula's been looking after you.
Frank Oh, yes. We had a nice little chat, as a matter of fact.

Paula gives him a look

James Hope you weren't waiting for vodka. (*He puts the vodka down on the drinks table*)
Frank No. I made a start on the whisky.
James Oh, splendid. (*He leads Susan across to Frank*) Now, you come over here a minute. Frank—you remember my daughter?

Frank looks at Susan with admiration

Frank Yes, I certainly do. I'd never have recognized you, though. But then you were only seven the last time I saw you.

They laugh

Well, this certainly *is* a surprise. James, you never said she was going to be here.

Susan He didn't know. I just rolled up like a bad penny. (*To James, playfully*) And nobody seems very pleased to see me. You know, I think I must have chosen a bad week-end . . .

James and Frank exchange a look

James Of course we're pleased to see you, darling.
Frank Yes. We certainly are!
James (*casually*) Oh, by the way, Frank—while I remember—there was a telephone call for you earlier on.

Frank turns, puzzled

Frank For *me*? *Here*?
James Yes.
Frank How extraordinary. What was it about?

Before James can reply the telephone rings

James Ah! That's probably for you now. (*He goes to the telephone and lifts the receiver*) Hullo? . . . Yes. . . . Yes, speaking . . . What? . . . Yes. But that's not possible . . . I beg your pardon? . . . *Where*? . . . When was this? . . . Yes. . . . Yes, of course I will. Right away. (*He hangs up*)

They are all looking at him. He turns to Paula

Paula What was that all about?
James You didn't lend my car to Mark tonight, did you?
Paula Yes. I did. Why?
James There's been an accident.
Paula Oh, no! Mark's all right, isn't he?

A dreadful pause

James I'm sorry, Paula. Mark's dead.

Paula turns to look at Frank. There is a second of total silence, then she screams loudly. The Lights snap to a Black-out, and—

the CURTAIN *falls*

ACT II

Scene 1

The same. Two hours later

It is starting to get dark outside. Frank is looking out into the night, smoking a small cigar. He turns as Susan comes in from the bedrooms

Frank How is she?
Susan About the same.
Frank Ghastly thing to happen . . .
Susan Yes. I just wish I could help her. (*She wanders towards the sofa*) She—she was very fond of Mark, you know.

Frank looks at her, surprised

Frank Yes. I know.

A pause. Susan sits on the edge of the sofa and looks anxiously at her wristwatch

Susan Isn't Daddy back from the police station yet? It must be two hours since he went.
Frank These things take time. A lot of formalities. You know how it is.
Susan I suppose so.

An awkward pause. Neither of them knows what to say. Frank wanders across to her, smoking his cigar

Frank Not much of a homecoming for you.
Susan (*with a wry smile*) No.

A pause

Frank Do you—do you see your father very often?
Susan Not as often as I'd like to. It's—difficult sometimes.

He looks at her, understanding what she means

Frank Yes. I suppose so. Still—he's luckier than I am. At least he's *got* you.

She smiles modestly

Susan Yes. (*Pause*) You still miss her, don't you? *Your* daughter.

He looks down and does not reply at once

Frank Yes. Quite a lot, as a matter of fact.

She reaches out and touches his hand sympathetically

Susan I'm sorry.

Frank Oh, I wouldn't want to forget her. I like to remember. It's just that sometimes I—I wish I could see her *now*. At your age. I miss that.

A pause. He drifts away

Susan Had she been ill for very long?

Frank turns

Frank Oh, she hadn't been ill.
Susan Then how . . . ?
Frank A car accident.
Susan Oh, no . . . !
Frank (*with a sigh*) Car going too fast. Sharp bend. Road a bit slippery. That was that.

A pause

Susan Was—was the driver killed as well?
Frank Oh, no. No. He was all right.

She has a sudden fear

Susan *You* weren't driving, were you?
Frank No, I wasn't there. A friend was giving her a lift to a party. (*Evasively*) It isn't important now. (*He puts his cigar out in the ashtray on the desk*)

Susan knows the answer in her heart before she asks

Susan Was it my father?

A pause. He looks down

Oh, my God—how awful for you.
Frank It wasn't very nice for James, either.

Paula comes in. She is pale and tired

Susan gets up and goes to her quickly

Susan Oh, Paula, you must try to rest.
Paula How can I, after what's happened?
Frank Well, come and sit down. Let me get you a drink.
Paula (*to Frank, sharply*) I don't want to sit down, for God's sake!
Susan Frank's only trying to help.
Paula Oh, yes. I'm sure he is! Frank's very good at helping, isn't he?

Susan glances at Frank, a little embarrassed by Paula's attitude to him

Susan I—er—I'll get you some coffee.

Susan goes out in awkward silence

Act II, Scene 1

Paula gets a cigarette from the armchair table and lights it, then she looks at Frank

Paula Well—you got the wrong one, didn't you, Frank?
Frank What are you talking about?
Paula You don't imagine that I think it was an accident, do you?
Frank Of course it was an accident!
Paula But what was it you said to me earlier this evening? "I've already made plans". Remember? Was this the plan you'd "already made"? You fixed James's car, was that it? Was that your plan? How appalled you must have been when you discovered that I'd lent the car to Mark! You've killed the wrong man, haven't you?

She turns away from him and sits on the sofa. Frank is rather alarmed. He moves in a little

Frank Paula—what happened was an accident. It has nothing to do with our conversation last night.

She faces him vehemently

Paula But isn't that what you said you were going to arrange? An accident to kill off my husband? I never for a moment thought you'd go through with it!

Silence. Frank goes to her, worried and anxious

Frank Now look—I know you're upset. And we all want to help you. But don't go accusing me of something I haven't done. If you go spreading wild rumours about things that aren't true, you'll only make everything worse, don't you see? (*He casts a nervous glance towards the door in case Susan should be coming back*) What we said to each other last night was between *us*. Between *us*, you understand? And no good can come of repeating it to other people. Especially the police.

Paula turns to look at him

Paula You're afraid, is that it? Afraid of the truth coming out?
Frank Don't be ridiculous! (*He turns away*)
Paula Afraid of what I'll say to the police?
Frank Oh, come on! Be sensible, Paula. (*Strongly*) Don't forget—*I* can talk, too!

They face each other

The front door opens and James comes in. He looks at them, sensing the slight atmosphere.

Frank breaks away from Paula. James closes the door

James Sorry I've been so long. The police kept me hanging about for ages. I thought I'd never get away. So many questions. (*He comes down the steps to Paula, concerned*) You all right, darling?
Paula Yes, James—I'm all right . . .

James exchanges a look with Frank, then moves round behind the sofa, lighting a cigarette

James The whole thing's so incredible, I—I can't believe it. I just can't believe it.
Frank Well—accidents do happen, James.

James looks at him

James Yes.
Paula If it *was* an accident.

James and Frank look at her

Susan comes in with a cup of coffee

Susan Oh, hullo, Daddy.
James Hullo, darling.

Susan moves to the sofa and hands the coffee to Paula

Susan Here you are, Paula. Nice strong coffee.
Paula Thank you. (*She takes the coffee and puts out her cigarette*)
Frank How did it happen, then, James?
James Well, I . . . (*He hesitates, looks at Paula, not wanting to upset her any more*)
Paula Go ahead. (*Sarcastically*) I'm sure Frank's longing to know exactly how it happened.

James and Susan react to her tone

James (*to Frank*) About three miles away. Just outside Cranston. There's a steep hill going down into the village.
Paula I should have thought Mark must have driven down a few steep hills before today. What was so special about this one, I wonder? Well? Go on, James. Why don't you tell us the rest?

James hesitates. Susan looks at Paula, puzzled

Susan What do you mean?
Paula (*to James*) Come on, darling. Don't keep us in suspense. Did the *police* think it was an accident, or is that just what *Frank* thinks?

A nasty silence. They all look at James. Finally he shakes his head regretfully

James No. It wasn't an accident.

They all react

Susan Wh-what do you mean?
Frank James, what are you talking about?
James Well—apparently the brake pipe had been cut.
Frank (*astonished*) Cut?
James Yes. It had been completely severed.
Frank You mean—deliberately?
James Yes. So after a few miles the brake fluid would have run out and

Act II, Scene 1

going down that steep hill into Cranston Mark wouldn't have had a chance.
Paula Oh, no . . .

Susan sits on the arm of the sofa, comforting Paula. Quite a pause

Frank But—*why?*
James I don't know, Frank. But whoever did it knew that the next time that car was used the person driving it would very probably be killed.

Dazed, Frank sits in the armchair. There is silence for a moment as they all digest this information

Susan I—I don't understand. You mean—somebody was actually trying to kill Mark?
James Well . . .
Susan But that's ridiculous!
Frank Isn't it possible they could have made a mistake? I mean, surely . . . ?
James No. I'm afraid there's no doubt at all.
Susan (*incredulously*) No doubt that somebody murdered Mark?
James That's what it looks like. And so—naturally—the police will be wanting to ask all of us some questions.

They all exchange looks

Frank You—you don't mean that the police think that one of *us* was trying to kill Mark?
James Well—not necessarily Mark.
Frank What do you mean?
James Well, as he was driving *my* car, I imagine they'll assume that whoever did it was trying to kill *me.*

Susan goes quickly to James

Susan You? Why should anyone want to kill you?
James (*with a wry smile*) I suppose there must be somebody who isn't quite as fond of me as you are, darling.
Susan (*starting to cry*) So if Mark hadn't borrowed the car, then you—you would have—*you* would have been . . . ! (*She starts to go, crying nervously*) I can't bear it! I just can't bear it! It might have been you! It might have been *you!*

Susan runs off to the bedrooms in tears

Frank rises to follow her

Frank Shall I go and . . . ?
James (*stopping him*) No, Frank. I—I think she'd prefer to be alone. For the time being.

A pause. Frank wanders towards the windows, lighting up another cigar. James turns to Paula

You knew, didn't you?

Paula I guessed.

James sits beside her sympathetically

James Darling, I—I really am sorry.
Paula It's all right, James. I'll be all right.

James looks across at Frank

James We were both very fond of Mark.
Frank Yes. I know.

James turns to Paula again

James Darling—what made you so certain that it wasn't an accident? You seemed so sure.

Frank looks anxiously at Paula

Paula I—I don't know. I suppose I just—felt it, that's all. (*To Frank, pointedly*) *You* didn't think it was an accident, either—did you, Frank?
Frank Of course I thought it was an accident!

Paula gives a small smile and turns again to James

Paula So is that what the police think, then? That somebody was trying to kill *you*?

James hesitates for a moment. He glances at Frank

James Er—well—no. *They* didn't say that. I'm only assuming that. After all, it's the obvious conclusion, isn't it? I mean—if somebody was planning to kill Mark, how could they be sure that he'd be driving my car?
Paula No. No, of course not. They couldn't have been ...
Frank Unless, of course, the murderer was the person who lent it to him.

Paula gets up, angrily

Paula What the hell do you mean by that? *I* lent it to him!
Frank Yes, Paula. That's exactly what I mean. I'm sorry, but nobody else but *you* knew that Mark would be driving the car.
James (*rising; appalled*) For God's sake, Frank—that's an outrageous suggestion!
Frank (*moving to James*) I'm sorry. I was only stating a fact. Look—we might all be suspected of murder. Isn't it better to discuss the facts amongst ourselves—before the *police* start asking questions? (*He ends up looking at Paula*)
James Well—yes, I suppose we ought to talk about it, but I can't understand why ...
Paula (*impatiently*) But surely *anyone* could have fixed the car, not necessarily one of *us*? It was sitting out there all night! Why should the police suspect *us*? (*She puts her coffee cup down on the sofa table*)
James I didn't say they *suspected* us! I said they'd want to ask questions!
Paula Well, I assumed that was what you meant.

Act II, Scene 1

James turns urgently to Frank, thinking hard

James Frank—I simply can't understand why you should think that Paula would want to kill Mark.
Paula Oh, for heaven's sake . . .
James I'm sorry, but I have a right to know. I want to know why Frank even suggested such a thing!

Paula looks at Frank. He sees the warning in her eyes and decides, for his own sake, not to proceed

Frank (*to James*) I—I don't know why I said that. It was stupid of me.
James But was it true?
Frank It really doesn't matter . . .
James (*moving towards Frank*) I think it does! I want to know why you should even *think* it, let alone *say* it.
Frank It isn't important!
Paula Yes. Let's just forget about it, shall we?
James No, we won't forget about it! (*To Frank*) You wanted to talk so let's talk! Why should you think Paula would want to kill Mark? (*No reply*) Well, come on—there must have been a reason.
Frank I—I don't know . . .
James You don't know? You practically accuse someone of murder and you say you don't know? You must have thought Paula had a *reason* to kill him, otherwise you wouldn't have mentioned it! I want to know what that reason was! (*A pause*) Well? Frank! *Well?*
Frank (*driven*) Well, perhaps he was becoming a bit of a nuisance to her!

A silence after the outburst. James looks at Paula. She does not catch his eye. He looks back at Frank

James A nuisance? What do you mean?
Frank (*reluctantly*) Well—persistent. You know. Boy-friends sometimes are.
James Boy-friends?
Frank (*with a sigh*) I'm sorry, James. But you would insist.
James (*after a moment*) I see. How stupid of me. (*He moves slowly to Paula*) All right, Paula. You may as well tell me. How *long* had you been having an affair with Mark?

Paula remains still, saying nothing

Paula! I want an answer! How long had it been going on?
Paula What the hell does that matter *now*?

She moves away from him to the sofa. He follows her

James How long had it been going on?
Paula It's none of your business! (*She escapes from him*)
James I think it's very much my business!

Paula turns on him below the sofa, like a cornered animal

Paula For God's sake, isn't it enough that he's dead? Isn't that enough? How do you think *I* feel? What does it matter how long it had been going on? It's over, isn't it? You needn't worry! I shan't be seeing him again!

Distressed, Paula sinks on to the sofa. A long pause. James looks at Frank, bewildered

James But how did *you* know about this, Frank?
Paula Oh, Frank's been quite the little private detective! Sneaking about in a shabby raincoat making a complete dossier of every bloody move I make!
James But *why*? (*To Frank*) Frank? Is this true?
Frank Not entirely. But I did know about Mark. She'd been seeing him for about six months.
James I see. (*He turns to Paula*) And *was* he being persistent? *Did* you want to get rid of him? (*No reply*) Paula—were you trying to end your affair with Mark?

Silence for a moment

Paula (*with difficulty*) I'm—I'm not sure. In a way I suppose I was. But not in the way you think. This isn't very easy for me, James.
James Nor for me.
Paula I—I wasn't—tired of him, if that's what you mean.
James (*bitterly*) Just frightened what *I* might find out?

She looks down, which James knows means "yes"

I see...

James moves towards the door to the bedrooms

Paula Where are you going?
James What the hell do *you* care?

James goes out abruptly, closing the door

Frank moves towards Paula

Frank So you really *were* trying to end your affair with Mark, then? And he wouldn't take no for an answer, eh? Was that it?
Paula (*flaring*) What if it was? You don't suppose I go around killing off boy-friends who won't take no for an answer? (*She gets up and goes to get another cigarette from the sofa table*) You know, it really wasn't very sensible of you to go and tell James about me and Mark. Because now there's no need for me to keep quiet about our conversation last night. I can tell James exactly what you suggested. *And* I can tell the police about your plan to kill him.
Frank And you think they'd believe you?

She looks at him directly

Paula We shall see, shan't we?

Frank holds her look for a moment, then smiles and moves away to the drinks table

Act II, Scene 1   51

Frank Oh, is it all right if I . . . ?
Paula (*abruptly*) Help yourself
Frank Thanks. (*He pours himself a whisky*)

A pause. Paula lights her cigarette and then looks thoughtfully at Frank

Paula Well? When did you do it, Frank?
Frank (vaguely) H'm? Do what?
Paula Fix the brakes, of course. When you arrived here for dinner tonight? You had plenty of opportunity. The car was out there in the drive, wasn't it?

Frank comes down with his drink, dismissing her suggestion with a smile

Frank It was daylight. Somebody might have seen me. (*He chuckles*) It's no good. You'll never pin this on me. (*He sits in the armchair*)
Paula (*thinking hard*) All right, then—if it wasn't tonight, it must have been *last* night. When it was dark and nobody was about. (*Moving to him*) Yes, of course! When I got back from dinner I saw you leaving here—and you saw me, didn't you, and you went off in the other direction! Don't you remember?
Frank Do me a favour! It was dark. You could have seen anybody.

Paula moves away thoughtfully

Paula I assumed that you'd been to see James, but *he* said you hadn't . . .

Frank looks surprised

Frank James said that?
Paula So why were you still prowling about outside at midnight? Perhaps *that* was when you did it?
Frank But wait a minute! I *did* come to see James last night.
Paula (*moving towards him*) He says you didn't.
Frank I can't imagine why. He must have forgotten. I definitely came back here.
Paula Well, we've only your word for that, haven't we? Anyway, even if you did you could have cut the brake pipe when you left. You had plenty of time.

A pause. She watches him, confident that she is right. Frank looks back at her with equal confidence

Frank Paula, you can accuse me as much as you like. But you'll never be able to prove it. Because I know I didn't do it. Oh, I suggested it, yes. I suggested it all right. But that isn't the same as actually *doing* it, is it?
Paula Then what reason will you give the police for coming here last night to see me when you knew James was out?

Frank smiles plausibly

Frank To blackmail you, of course. You didn't really think I came for any other reason, did you? I only talked about murder to up the ante. I mean, why should I want James dead? He's been a good friend to me over the years. Helped me financially when I was down on my luck. No. The police would see that I had no reason to kill him. Whereas—let's face it, Paula—you had, hadn't you?

Paula holds his look for a moment, then starts to laugh, moving away

Paula You know, you really must make up your mind. A moment ago you were suggesting that I had tried to kill *Mark*—now you say it was *James* I was trying to kill!

Frank's thoughts are racing as he tries to keep one step ahead. He rises and moves slowly towards her

Frank Well, Paula—you see, it is possible, isn't it, that after I'd gone last night, and you and Mark were having dinner together, that you started to think about my plan to kill James. And—well—maybe you decided it wasn't such a bad idea after all. Only why include *me* when you could just as easily do it all on your own?

A pause. Paula looks at him with a mocking smile

Paula I see. So you think I fixed the car to kill James?

He shrugs expansively

Frank Well, it's possible, isn't it?
Paula And then sent *Mark* out in it, knowing that *he'd* be the one who was killed? Really, Frank! You'll have to do better than that. (*She turns away from him*)

James comes in

Frank goes to meet him

Frank Is Susan all right?
James Yes. I think so. Poor kid.
Paula (*icily*) Isn't it time you went home, Frank? Or are you intending to stay with us for ever? (*She sits on the sofa*)
James Paula . . . !

James and Frank exchange a look

Frank I was just going, anyway. (*He finishes off his whisky*)
James If the police want to contact you tonight I'll give them your phone number. Is that all right?
Frank Yes. Of course. (*He puts his empty glass down on the armchair table*) Oh, by the way, I don't suppose you remember who it was who telephoned me?
James (*blankly*) Telephoned you?
Frank Yes. You started to tell me about it, and then we—then we heard the news about the accident.
James Good Lord, yes—I'd forgotten all about it. Let me see now. I don't think they said who it was. I simply told them you weren't here at the moment.

Act II, Scene 1

Frank (*thoughtfully*) I can't imagine who would be ringing me *here* . . .
James Well, it doesn't matter, does it? Whoever it was said they'd ring you on Monday.
Frank Oh—fine. Well, I'll—I'll just go and say good-bye to Susan.

Frank glances at Paula and then goes out

Silence. James goes to Paula

James (*gently*) I—I'm sorry I went on a bit just now. I do know what you must be going through.

Paula takes his hand affectionately, genuinely sorry

Paula I'm sorry, too. I—I didn't want you to find out. Not like that.
James Was it—*was* it all over? Between you and Mark?

A pause. She considers

Paula Yes. Yes, it was. (*Pause*) It—wasn't really very serious, anyway.

James looks down sadly

James That's no consolation.

She looks at him sympathetically

Paula I'm sorry.

He just gives a little smile

James Oh, well . . . (*He wanders away. After a pause*) Had Frank *really* been watching you? Spying on you?

A brief pause

Paula Er—I—I don't know.
James But that's what you said.
Paula (*evasively*) I—I was angry. I didn't know what I was saying.
James I mean—why would Frank want to *do* that?
Paula I probably imagined it.
James And yet he knew about Mark . . .
Paula Well, he met Mark last night. Before we went to dinner.
James (*relieved*) Oh, I see. Oh, well, that's all right, then. I couldn't really see Frank doing anything like that. Not spying on someone. (*He goes to get a drink*) Drink?
Paula No, thanks. I wish I understood why you always defend Frank.
James I'm sorry for him.
Paula You shouldn't be.
James Why not? He's an old friend, and he hasn't exactly had his share of good fortune, you know.
Paula (*flaring*) I'll tell you why you shouldn't feel sorry for him. Because it was Frank who fixed your car! It was Frank who was trying to kill you!

James returns with his whisky

James Darling, don't be ridiculous! Frank's one of my oldest friends. We worked together twenty years ago. What makes you think he was trying to kill me, for heaven's sake?
Paula Because he told me.

A brief pause. He looks at her incredulously

James *Told* you?
Paula Last night. That's what he came here to talk to me about!

He goes and sits beside her

James (*lightly, with a smile*) Isn't that just a little unlikely, darling? If you're going to kill somebody, I wouldn't have thought you'd go and tell the chap's wife all about it.
Paula He hoped that I'd agree to his suggestion!
James Oh, I see—he wanted you to co-operate with him in killing me off? (*He laughs*) Really, darling—I know you don't like Frank, but you can't expect me to believe a story like that!
Paula It's the truth!
James But why should he think for a moment that you'd agree to such a thing?
Paula (*with difficulty*) Because—because of what he knew about Mark.
James (*lightly*) He could hardly think that you'd agree to having me bumped off simply because of one brief love affair. (*A pause*) Or—or were there *other* men that Frank knew about?

Paula rises restlessly and moves away

Paula No—no, of course not!
James Then I can't see how he could possibly think you'd be interested in the proposition. (*With a kindly smile*) Darling, it really doesn't make sense.

She turns to face him

Paula It's what he said! Here in this room!
James (*thoughtfully*) Then in that case you'd better tell the police.
Paula (*uncertainly*) Yes. Yes, I suppose so . . . But the trouble is that then he'll tell them about *me*.
James You said there was nothing much to tell.
Paula Yes, but—well—you know—exaggerated stories—invented stories! Stories that would harm *me*! (*She returns to him*) And I wouldn't want that, James. I wouldn't want that.

He watches her steadily for a moment, and knows that she is lying

James (*quietly*) It wasn't *just* Mark, was it? (*A pause. Loudly*) *Was* it?
Paula *No!* No, no . . . (*She moves away to the armchair*)
James And Frank *had* been watching you?
Paula Apparently. Yes.
James I see. (*Pause*) So we can forget all about his plan for murdering me, then, can't we?

Act II, Scene 1   55

Paula What do you mean?
James Frank was going to blackmail you. Was that it?
Paula No—no!
James Perhaps he was blackmailing you already. And if he was he'd hardly want me out of the way, would he? Otherwise he'd be throwing away his trump card. You can't threaten to reveal secrets to a dead man.

Paula sits wearily in the armchair

Paula But he *wasn't* blackmailing me!
James (*continuing inexorably*) Well, in any event, I shouldn't tell the police about your conversation with Frank.
Paula Why not?
James Because—don't you see?—it would give *you* a reason for wanting *me* out of the way!

She looks at him in horror

Paula You don't think that I . . . ?
James Well, how do you think it would look to the police?
Paula But it's what *you* think, too, isn't it?
James I didn't say that!
Paula (*rising agitatedly*) You think I wanted to kill you?
James I'm telling you what the police might think. It would be natural for them to assume that if Frank was threatening to tell me things about your private life—things that I might find it hard to forgive—then you'd be glad to have me out of the way! God knows you'd be a very rich widow!

Paula breaks away from him, distressed

Paula But Frank *wasn't* blackmailing me! He came here to talk about murder. (*She turns to face him again*) Don't you believe me?

James follows her wearily

James Paula, I don't know *what* to believe . . .
Paula (*flaring*) If I *had* been planning to kill you, I would hardly lend the car to my lover, knowing that he was almost certainly going to his death! (*She turns away from him*)

There is quite a pause, then James speaks, watching her carefully

James But if what you say is true—if Frank *had* come here to talk about murder—you might have agreed to his plan, but now known that he had already set that plan in motion.

She gazes at him for a moment in disbelief, then goes to him

Paula You really *do* believe it. Don't you know me better than that?
James After tonight I'm beginning to wonder if I know you at all.

Paula moves away, then decides to counter-attack and turns to face him

Paula All right. All right—you've asked *me* a lot of questions—now it's

my turn! Why did you say that Frank didn't come back here to see you last night when I was out?
James Because he didn't.
Paula He says that he did.
James Then he was mistaken.
Paula (*with sudden suspicion*) What did he want to see you about? I think it's *you* who are up to something! What the hell was going on here last night?
James Paula, for heaven's sake! Nothing was going on.
Paula You're always very keen to defend Frank, aren't you? Perhaps it's really you and Frank who have been planning something!
James (*wearily*) Darling—believe me—I didn't see him last night.

Frank comes in

Paula Ah! Frank—you're just in time.

Frank comes down between them, looking a little puzzled

Now perhaps you can decide which of you is telling the truth.

Frank looks at James, then back at Paula

Frank The truth? What about?
Paula About whether you came back here last night after Mark and I had left.

Frank looks at James, undecided

Well?
James (*holding Frank's look*) *I* don't remember it, Frank. Do you?

Frank hesitates

Frank Well... (*He smiles guiltily at Paula*) Well, I—I didn't actually *see* him, no. I rang the doorbell but he didn't answer.

Paula gazes at him uncomprehendingly

James I was probably in the bath.
Frank (*to Paula*) You see, after I left you and Mark, I went down to the pub and had a few drinks. So on my way home I thought I'd look in and see if James was back yet.
Paula But you didn't see him?
Frank No.
Paula (*bewildered*) I don't understand. First you say you saw him. Now you say you didn't. Why have you changed your mind?
Frank I haven't. (*Evasively*) It—it was a misunderstanding.

Paula looks suspiciously from James to Frank

Paula You two are up to something, aren't you?
James Oh, Paula—for heaven's sake...
Paula So what did you do, Frank?
Frank When?

Act II, Scene 1

Paula When James didn't answer the door.
Frank I went home, of course.
Paula No, you didn't! You were still outside when I got back at midnight. What were you doing all that time?
Frank (*moving to Paula*) I told you—it wasn't *me* you saw!
Paula We've only got your word for that, haven't we?

James intervenes hastily

James Look, I think we've all said enough for tonight. Let's just leave it, shall we?
Frank (*his eyes fixed on Paula*) Not yet, James, if you don't mind. There's something *I* want to talk about. Something important.
James Look—Paula's tired. She must get some rest. I really think you ought to go.

James takes Frank's arm and tries to urge him on his way, but Frank pulls away from him roughly

Frank No! You wait a minute!
James Frank, I want you to go!
Frank Not yet! You asked me earlier why I should think that Paula would want to kill Mark . . .
James (*firmly*) Frank—I said we'd had enough . . .!
Frank Well, I've just been talking to Susan!
James What the hell's that got to do with it? Whatever you and Susan talked about can't make any difference to what's happened.
Frank I wouldn't be too sure about that.
James I don't understand what the hell you're talking about!
Frank Oh, you will in a minute, James . . .
Paula For God's sake get him out of here!
Frank You see, the point is—did Paula have a reason for wanting Mark out of the way? Did she have a motive for killing him?
James What's that got to do with Susan?
Frank Well, Susan arrived here unexpectedly today, didn't she?
James Yes, I know that, but . . .
Frank She arrived unexpectedly—and overheard a rather interesting conversation. Didn't she, Paula?
Paula Oh, for God's sake! (*She moves away dismissively*)
James What conversation? What the hell are you talking about?

Frank looks triumphantly across at Paula

Frank What conversation, Paula?

James looks at Paula

James What conversation, Paula?
Paula (*wearily*) A conversation between me and Mark . . .

Frank smiles delightedly

Frank Exactly! And Susan's just been telling me all about it.

James turns to Frank again

James I think you'd better come to the point.
Frank Mark was wanting to tell you about his affair with Paula. He wanted you to know all about it and for you to divorce Paula. She was anxious to prevent this happening—for very obvious, financial reasons.

There is a pause as James digests this information, then he turns to Paula

James Is this true? *Did* Mark want to tell me?
Paula (*coldly*) I'm sure your precious daughter has an excellent memory.

(*She turns away*)

James I see . . . (*He moves away thoughtfully to the windows*)

Paula moves to Frank, her eyes blazing

Paula And you honestly believe that I decided there and then to kill Mark by lending him James's car and fixing the brakes?
Frank Well, you had good reason. As we now know. (*He sits on the sofa confidently*)
Paula But haven't you forgotten something?
Frank I don't think so. What?
Paula I didn't even know that Mark was going to stay for dinner, did I? Or that he'd insist on going home to change. So how could I have known that I'd have the opportunity to lend him the car? (*She moves closer to him*) And when do you suppose I fixed the brakes? H'm? (*Carefully and triumphantly*) I never went out of this room from the time Mark arrived until he left in the car!

This rather takes the wind out of Frank's sails. He looks at her for a moment

Frank Are you *sure* of that?
Paula Absolutely certain. And, as we all agree, the only person who could have arranged to kill Mark would have had to know he was going to use the car, *and* have the opportunity to fix the brakes. So you'll have to think of something else, won't you? (*She turns away from him dismissively*)

James turns from the windows and looks at Frank

James (*coldly*) If you're satisfied now, Frank, I'd like you to go.

Frank holds his look for a moment

Frank Yes. Yes, of course. I'm sorry. (*He gets up to go, then hesitates and turns to Paula again*) So only you and Mark were here when he decided to go home and change for dinner?
Paula (*defiantly*) Yes.

Frank starts to go, then Paula has a sudden thought

No—wait a minute . . .!

Frank and James look at her

Act II, Scene 1

James What is it?
Paula Well—only that Susan was here as well. *She* knew Mark was going home to change.
Frank Susan?
Paula Yes.

James looks horrified and moves quickly to Paula

James You're not suggesting that—that *Susan* . . . ?
Paula I'm saying she was the only other person in the room at the time.
James But she'd never do a thing like that!
Frank Of course not! And apart from anything else—when could she have fixed the brakes on the car? Presumably *she* didn't have the opportunity any more than you did?
Paula Well—yes, as a matter of fact, she did.
James (*appalled*) What do you mean?
Paula I remember now. She'd left her things in her car and she went out to get them—just before Mark left.
Frank So she could have cut the brake pipe then?
Paula Why not? (*To James, astringently*) Or perhaps they don't teach you that sort of thing at car maintenance classes?
James I—I just can't believe that you're even suggesting such a thing! Why should Susan want to kill Mark? It doesn't make sense! (*Appealing to Frank*) Frank—tell her!

A pause. Frank looks uncertain

Frank Well—I dunno about that.
James (*appalled*) What?
Frank Well, I mean—Susan's very fond of you, isn't she? Very loving. Devoted. Maybe she saw Mark as a threat to your happiness. She could have been trying to protect you. It's not unusual to want to protect the person you love most.

James looks from one to the other in horror

James How can you even suggest such a thing? Can you really imagine a kid like Susan planning to kill somebody? What's the matter with you both?
Paula (*flaring*) It was you who said we were all under suspicion. *All* of us! Or does that exclude Susan because she happens to be your loving daughter?

James stares at her angrily, his chest heaving, then he turns and goes quickly out of the room

Paula starts to follow him, regretting what she has said

James! I'm sorry . . . !

But James has gone. Paula turns to see Frank looking at her doubtfully

Frank You don't really believe all that, do you? About Susan.

Paula (*with a shrug*) Well, it's possible, isn't it? (*She gets a cigarette from the armchair table*)
Frank Not very probable, though. You'd *like* to believe it, wouldn't you? And you'd like *us* to believe it. Because it would take the suspicion away from you.
Paula (*reasonably*) Well, if someone *was* trying to kill Mark—as *you* suggested—then Susan is the only one who had the opportunity. (*She sits in the armchair and lights her cigarette*)
Frank Unless you'd already fixed the brakes to kill James—and then decided to kill Mark instead because suddenly he was threatening to rock the boat. (*He grins sheepishly*) It would be so much easier, wouldn't it, if only we knew who the intended victim really was? Was it James? Or was it Mark? (*Going to her eagerly*) Let's just look at all the possibilities, shall we?

Paula gives him a patient, long-suffering look and agrees

Paula You want to play games—all right, go ahead.
Frank One: Susan was trying to kill Mark. Possible. Motive—fair. Not exactly a front runner, though. Two: *you* wanted to kill Mark. Again possible. Motive—good.
Paula But no opportunity.
Frank No. Unless you changed your target at the last minute. H'm. Bit of an outsider, though, eh? Three: you and I were trying to kill James *together*. But we both know that you hadn't agreed to that, don't we?
Paula So that leaves only two alternatives.
Frank Exactly.
Paula Either *I* was trying to kill James. Or *you* were trying to kill James. And I know it wasn't me.

He looks steadily at her

Frank (*quietly*) And *I* know it wasn't *me* . . .

Pause. He turns away from her

Paula So one of us is lying.
Frank Yes.

Pause

Or we're both telling the truth.

She looks at him

In which case there's only one possible explanation. (*He looks at her*) James did it himself.

Paula stares at him incredulously

Paula Cut the brake pipe on his own car? If he'd wanted to commit suicide there are easier ways than that.
Frank I didn't mean suicide. Suppose—just suppose—that at that time James already knew about you and Mark.

Act II, Scene 2

Paula But he didn't! Not then.
Frank Suppose he did?
Paula Then why should he fix the brakes on his own car? He couldn't possibly have known that I was going to lend the car to Mark. (*She suddenly remembers something and looks horrified*) Oh, my God ...!
Frank What's the matter?
Paula I've just remembered—I was going out early tomorrow morning. But I hadn't got *my* car because James didn't collect it for me after all. So he said—that I could borrow *his* ...

Frank sees the possible truth and slowly puts it into words

Frank So James knew that the next person to drive *his* car—would be *you*.

Paula looks at Frank with dreadful realization as the Lights fade to a Black-out, and—

the CURTAIN *falls*

SCENE 2

The same. The following morning

It is a bright, sunny day. The garden doors are open

James is sitting in the armchair, still and thoughtful. After a moment Frank appears in the garden. James does not notice him. He looks in through the garden doors

Frank All right if I come in?

James comes out of his reverie, and looks up

James Oh, hullo, Frank. Yes, of course.

Frank comes into the room

Frank Paula not about?
James She went for a walk. Felt like a breath of air.
Frank Nice morning for it. Sun shining. Do her the world of good.

Frank looks at James appraisingly, as if trying to sum him up. James looks up and catches him

  I don't suppose you managed to get much sleep.
James Not much. No.
Frank Nor me. Too many things to think about.

James looks at him briefly, a little puzzled

James Yes. (*He sighs heavily and gets up*) I know it's a bit early but I need a drink. Join me?
Frank Good idea!
James Scotch?

Frank Fine.

James goes to pour two whiskies. Frank again watches him carefully

How long had you known about Paula?

There is a pause. James does not turn

James Probably a lot longer than you have.

Frank gives a knowing smile

Frank Yes. I thought it didn't come as a great surprise to you last night. (*He sits on the sofa*)
James Oh, dear. Was it as obvious as that?
Frank Only to me.
James About a year, I suppose. You see, *I* was getting pretty good at detective work, too. And *I* wasn't even trying.

James arrives with the whiskies and gives one to Frank

Frank Thanks. Cheers.
James Cheers.

They drink. James looks at Frank steadily

Now you tell *me* something. Why did you decide to blackmail Paula?

A pause. Frank holds his look calmly

Frank You really don't know? I saw her quite by chance in a restaurant. And she wasn't with you. They seemed—content together. And then I happened to see her again with the same man. I needed more money. As you know. So it seemed like a good idea.
James And you started following her. Watching her. Making notes.

Frank shrugs

Frank Well, I had to have evidence, didn't I?

James drifts away with his drink

Why aren't you angry?

James shrugs

James We all have to make a living. (*Disparagingly*) Presumably that was the only way you knew.
Frank (*with a slight edge*) But I didn't have your luck, did I, James?
James Luck? Is that what it was?

A pause. Frank is watching James intently, trying to sort something out in his own mind

Frank By the way—that telephone call that came for me yesterday—sorry to go on about it, but—are you *sure* there wasn't a message?

James looks at him, then wanders away to the windows

Act II, Scene 2

James Yes. Quite sure. I told you. Why? Do you think it was important?
Frank I'm just curious to know who it was, that's all.
James If it was important presumably they'll ring again.
Frank Yes. I suppose so.

They drink in silence for a moment. James looks out into the garden

Must have been a terrible shock for you. When you first found out about Paula.
James Yes ...
Frank Didn't you ever think of leaving her?
James Two or three times a day at first.
Frank Why didn't you talk to her about it?

James turns from the windows

James What good would that have done?
Frank At least she'd have known how you felt.

James moves restlessly down to the desk

James And you think that would have made any difference?
Frank So you just put up with it? Hating her more and more every day.

A silence

James I don't remember saying that I hated her.
Frank But—surely—you must have done!

James smiles wryly

James I never for a moment contemplated the idea of murdering her, if that's what you're leading up to. (*He looks at Frank*)

Frank shrugs

Frank Nobody would have blamed you if you had.
James (*going to Frank*) Oh, I dunno. It was probably my fault anyway. Perhaps I'm not as easy to live with as I imagined. Anyway, it never occurred to me. (*He sees Frank looking doubtful*) Or don't you believe me?
Frank Well, after all, you could have fixed the car yourself, couldn't you?
James (*puzzled*) But *why*?
Frank Because you knew that Paula was going to use it this morning.

A brief pause

James *Was* she?
Frank Yes. You'd promised to lend her your car. Don't you remember?
James Good Lord, yes! I'd forgotten all about that.
Frank So you could have planned to kill her out of jealousy. Crime of passion, I think they call it. Very popular on the Continent.

They look at each other for a moment

James You don't really believe that.

A pause. Then Frank shakes his head

Frank No. I did last night. For a moment. But I don't any more.

James holds Frank's look for a moment, slightly puzzled, then moves away

James The trouble is, you see—I still love Paula. In spite of Mark. In spite of all the others.

Frank looks at him in surprise

Frank You knew about *them*, too?
James Oh, yes. I knew. But I suppose I always lived in the hope that one day we'd be—as we used to be. And I wouldn't want to lose the chance of that.

Susan comes in from the bedrooms and sees Frank

Susan Oh. Oh, hullo, Frank. I—I didn't know you were here.
Frank (*rising*) Just arrived.
Susan Can I get you some coffee?
Frank No, thanks. (*He holds up his glass of whisky*)
Susan Ah...
Frank (*with a smile*) It was your father's idea. Blame him.

The telephone rings. James goes and lifts the receiver

James (*on the telephone*) Hullo? ... Yes, speaking ... Yes? ... Yes, there were a few things in the glove compartment. And a rug or something in the boot. Nothing important, though ... What—*now*? Well, I don't really mind. I can easily pick them up—tomorrow—anytime. ... Oh. ... Oh, I see. (*He looks at his watch*) Er—yes—well, I suppose so. If you feel it's necessary. ... Very well. I'll come over right away, then. Good-bye.

James puts the receiver down, looking puzzled

How extraordinary...
Susan Who was it?
James It was the police. They want me to collect the bits and pieces that I'd left in the car. I can't think why they're making such a fuss. There's nothing very valuable. Still, they want me to go, so I'd better go. (*To Susan*) Would you ring a taxi for me, darling?
Susan There's no need. I'll drive you there.
James (*pleased*) Will you? Oh—fine. I'd forgotten you'd got a car now. You sure you don't mind?
Susan Of course not.
James Oh, splendid! I'll just go and get my jacket. Shan't be a minute.

James goes

Frank resumes his seat

Frank You'll spoil him.
Susan (*with a smile*) He deserves it.

Act II, Scene 2

Frank Yes. Yes, I'm sure he does.

A pause

Susan I—I feel awful about the things I told you last night. About Paula and Mark.
Frank There's no need to.
Susan It was just that—well, I felt sorry for Daddy. I know I shouldn't have listened. And it upset me, hearing it all. But it *was* wrong of me to tell you.
Frank Forget it. It really isn't important.
Susan No. I suppose it isn't. Not now.

A pause

Frank Susan . . .
Susan Yes?
Frank Will you take a bit of advice from an old man?
Susan (*smiling*) Depends what it is. And you're not old.
Frank Don't ever get *too* fond of one person. It can put far too much responsibility on them. And sometimes it can make you see things in a distorted way. Out of proportion. And that can be dangerous.
Susan You think I love my father too much?
Frank It's possible.
Susan Do *you* think you loved your *daughter* too much?

He considers

Frank Yes. Yes, perhaps I did. If I'd loved her a little less, it might have made it easier for me.

They look at each other for a moment, then Susan feels she has gone too far

Susan Oh, dear. I shouldn't have said *that,* either! I'm very sorry.

Paula comes in from the garden

Paula What are you sorry about?
Frank (*rising*) Good morning, Paula.
Paula Hullo, Frank . . .
Frank I—I thought I'd come over.

Paula looks at him

Paula I'm glad you did.

A brief pause, as Paula and Frank look at each other, then Paula turns to Susan

What are you sorry about?
Susan (*reluctantly*) Oh—er—nothing. We were—just talking about . . . (*She peters out uncertainly*)
Frank About my daughter.
Paula (*sympathetically*) Oh. Yes. Yes, that was very sad . . .
Susan You knew about it, then?

Paula Oh, yes. Frank told me.
Susan Wasn't it dreadful that Daddy of all people should be driving the car?

A brief pause

Paula What do you mean?
Susan Oh. Didn't you know that?
Paula No.
Susan Oh. (*to Frank*) I'm sorry, Frank.
Paula (*to Frank*) James—was driving the car?
Frank Yes.
Paula No. I didn't know that. (*She turns away thoughtfully*)
Susan (*to Frank*) Oh, dear—I assumed she would have known ...
Frank Look, it doesn't matter—it's a long time ago. Let's forget all about it, shall we?

James comes in. He is ready to go, with his tie and jacket on

James Right. I'm ready. (*He sees Paula*) Oh, hullo, darling.
Paula Where are you going?
James The police want me to collect my belongings from the car.
Paula Couldn't they have given them to you last night when you were there?
James I'd have thought so. And anyway, there's no hurry for them. Can't think what they're making such a fuss about. Still, Susan's driving me, so we shan't be long.

James and Susan start to go

Paula Look what I found!

James and Susan stop and look at her

James What?

Paula holds up some car keys

Paula My car keys.
James Where were they?
Paula In the boot of my car. Exactly where George said he'd leave them.
James Well, they weren't there last night.
Paula You can't have looked properly.
James (*sheepishly*) Sorry, darling. I thought I'd looked everywhere. Anyway, you've got your car back now. That's the main thing.
Paula Yes.
James Right, Sue—off we go!
Susan See you later!
Frank And, Susan—remember what I said.
Susan (*with a smile*) I'll try.

James and Susan go off into the garden

Paula follows them to the windows and watches them go, then looks at Frank. A silence. Frank goes to refill his drink

Act II, Scene 2

Paula Are you drinking already?
Frank Yes. I'm afraid so. Want one?
Paula No, thanks. (*She moves towards the sofa, restlessly*)
Frank (*pouring his drink*) Well, it makes a change for you to be glad to see me.
Paula Yes. Sometimes one finds oneself with doubtful allies. (*She lights a cigarette*)

Frank returns with his drink, deep in thought, working something out in his mind

Frank Funny, James not finding your car keys.
Paula Yes.
Frank He's not usually so unobservant.
Paula (*with a smile*) You don't know James.

He looks directly at her

Frank Do *you*?

Paula holds his look for a moment, then she sits thoughtfully on the sofa

Paula I'm not sure ... (*Pause*) After our conversation I was awake all night. I kept—looking at him. Wondering. It's a weird feeling to be in a room with somebody you think might have tried to kill you. (*Pause*) Not that you could blame him after what I've done. The ridiculous thing is that—that I love James. I didn't want to hurt him. But I—I just *wanted* Mark. Especially Mark ...

A pause

Frank (*quietly*) Well, if it's any consolation to you, I don't think that he did.
Paula What?
Frank Try to kill you. If James had wanted to do that he could have fixed the brakes on *your* car, couldn't he?
Paula Yes. Yes, I suppose so. (*Puzzled*) But that isn't what you thought last night.

Frank drifts away to the armchair

Frank No. I know. But this morning I don't think he was trying to kill you. (*He drinks some of his whisky*)
Paula This morning? Why are you so certain this morning?
Frank Because *I* didn't sleep last night, either. Too busy thinking.
Paula Well, I hope you're right. I couldn't really believe that James would ... (*She peters out*) So we still don't know what really happened, do we?
Frank No. Not for sure ... (*He wanders away, his mind racing*)

Paula watches him, thoughtfully. There is quite a pause

Paula I didn't know that James was driving the car when your daughter was killed.

Frank stops, his back to her, looking out of the windows

Frank Does it make any difference? Who was driving.
Paula It might.

He turns to look at her

Frank What do you mean?
Paula How you must have hated him going on and on about his wonderful clever daughter after what he'd done to *yours*!
Frank That isn't fair. It wasn't James's fault. He was heartbroken over what happened. (*He moves down towards the desk*)
Paula Yes. I'm sure he was. And I'm sure he'd want to repay you for what he'd done. (*She rises and moves to the armchair, her eyes on him*) Was he sending you money all the time you lived in Australia?

Frank is surprised at the suggestion

Frank No! No, of course not! (*He crosses away below the sofa*)
Paula Are you sure?
Frank (*vehemently*) Of course I'm sure! I didn't ask him for any money, and he didn't send any money!
Paula Didn't send any money to Australia?
Frank No! I didn't even write to him from Australia!

A pause

Paula Oh. Oh, I see ...

Paula's thoughts are racing, her suspicion of Frank rekindled

Perhaps that's the answer, then?
Frank (*puzzled*) What?
Paula All the time you were in Australia you kept thinking about what had happened to your daughter. Until in the end you couldn't stand it any longer. So you came back to England for one reason—to kill James! Out of revenge!

Frank looks at her with a cynical smile

Frank Oh, my God. It didn't take you long to start accusing *me* again, did it?
Paula (*going to him; urgently*) Only because I want to know the truth! I must know the *truth*!
Frank (*loudly*) Then for God's sake listen!

Silence. Then Frank speaks calmly and precisely

I came back to England because I wasn't much of a success in Australia. Yes, I needed money. I'd tried. And failed. And I needed money. And I thought James might help me. And he did.
Paula Every time you asked him?
Frank (*carefully*) Whenever he was able to. Now listen—there's something I ...

Act II, Scene 2

Paula So ever since you got back from Australia you've been pressing James for money, hoping that his conscience about your daughter would always force him to pay up?

Frank moves away angrily

Frank I told you—James helped me whenever he was able to!

She follows him, still searching desperately for the truth

Paula Was that what you came back here last night to see him about? To ask for more money?

Frank (*moving away from her*) James said he didn't see me last night, don't you remember?

Paula (*following him*) Perhaps he was lying. Covering up for you! Protecting you—like he always does. Suppose you *did* see him last night, and you asked for more and he said no he couldn't afford it? No more money—not *ever*! So with that—and the memory of the car accident that killed your daughter—you decided to kill James!

Frank Paula, will you please let me . . .!

Paula (*continuing inexorably*) And how very apt, you thought, for *James* to die in a car accident just as *she* did! Only this time it wasn't an accident. So when you left, you made sure nobody was looking and you quickly cut through the brake pipe on his car, and you were leaving the garden when you saw me getting out of a taxi, so you turned quickly and went off the other way, hoping that I hadn't seen you! That's what really happened—(*desperately*)—isn't it, Frank?

Frank (*loudly*) No, it isn't! And if you'll just listen for a minute, I'll tell you what I think *did* happen!

A pause. Breathing heavily, Paula looks at him for a moment

Paula What do you mean? You—know something?

Frank Yes. I think I do. (*He finishes off his whisky and goes to pour another. He also pours one for her*) Just now you said you weren't sure if you really knew your husband. Well, there *is* something you don't know about him. (*He returns to her with the drinks and hands one to her*) Here— you'd better have one, too.

She takes the whisky

I know things about James.

Paula What do you mean? What things?

Frank Things that could put him in prison. For quite a long time.

Paula looks at him incredulously

Paula James? In prison? Don't be ridiculous! (*She moves to the armchair, dismissing the idea*)

Frank I don't suppose he ever told you what really happened to that firm of ours all those years ago?

Paula It was all over and forgotten long before I met him.

Frank So he never had to explain to you how a pretty prosperous firm like ours suddenly went bust?
Paula I assumed—the changing market. Lack of demand. It happens to the best people. And to the best companies.

Frank plays his trump card

Frank So does embezzlement.

A long pause. Then Paula laughs

Paula Embezzlement? Oh, come on! Don't be ridiculous. (*She sits in the armchair with her drink*)
Frank Oh, you don't think that dear, upright, honest James would stoop to a thing like that?
Paula Why should he? He was a successful man.
Frank Yes, but you see—James does make the mistake of always marrying women with expensive tastes.
Paula You mean Lisa?
Frank Exactly. Some men never learn, do they? So James had been taking a little bit here and a little bit there. To give Lisa the things that she wanted. The things she couldn't do without.
Paula Well, you can hardly blame the collapse of the firm on the loss of a little petty cash!
Frank Oh, I wouldn't call it petty. James had been fiddling the books to the tune of thirty-five thousand pounds. And that was a hell of a lot of money in those days.
Paula (*sceptically*) Then why wasn't he found out?
Frank Because he was far too clever. Nobody ever knew.
Paula *You* knew.
Frank Oh, yes. I knew. Because, believe it or not, in those days *I* was as clever as James. So clever that I even kept copies of the evidence.
Paula I wouldn't call that clever. I'd call it cunning.
Frank Call it what you like. I've got the proof.
Paula Why didn't you use it at the time? Why keep quiet and disappear to Australia?
Frank Because I was young, I suppose. And honest. And believed in friendship. All those things. Also in those days I still had a little pride... I was determined to succeed on my own. Oh, I tried, Paula. Believe me, I tried very hard. But, unlike James, who could start all over again and succeed—with the help of the thirty-five thousand pounds of course!— I failed.

She rises, angrily

Paula And that's why you returned to England and came here? To collect!
Frank To ask for help.
Paula To blackmail him!
Frank Oh, I wouldn't call it that, Paula. I really did feel that some of that thirty-five thousand should have been mine. And, make no mistake, James was very understanding. Not pleased, but understanding. (*Going

Act II, Scene 2

to her) So, Paula—ask yourself this. How often does a man try to kill the goose that is, even occasionally, laying a golden egg?

Paula moves away from him up to the windows. She is still puzzled, unsure of what he is up to

Paula But—why are you telling me all this?

He goes to her, urgently

Frank Because I want you to be quite certain that I didn't try to kill James. I really didn't, Paula. He was far too useful to me. Anyway, I don't think I'd have made a success of *that*, either. I don't think I'd have had the guts. *I* didn't try to kill him. Any more than *you* did.

She turns and looks at him for a moment

Paula Oh, so you're sure of *that* now, are you?
Frank Yes. I am.
Paula Why?
Frank Because I think I know what *really* happened.

Paula holds his look for a moment, then moves away from him nervously

Paula What do you mean?
Frank It all came to me suddenly last night when I got back to my digs, and found that yesterday—somebody had telephoned me.
Paula Is that so unusual?
Frank (*going to her*) Whoever it was didn't leave his name. But he did leave a message. An *urgent* message.
Paula (*bewildered*) What about?
Frank About my mother.

Paula looks at him uncomprehendingly

Paula Your mother?
Frank Yes. She's a dear old thing. Very independent. Lives all alone. And I'm—very fond of her. I'd hate to see—anything happen to her.

A pause, then Paula speaks quietly

Paula What did the message say?
Frank It said that my "dear old mother" was dangerously ill. And would I go to her at once. *As quickly as possible.*

Paula looks puzzled

Paula Well—didn't the people at your digs know where you were?
Frank Oh, yes. I'd left them this number.
Paula So why didn't they let you know?
Frank Oh, they tried to. They rang here. (*A brief pause*) And spoke to James. They told *him* about my mother. But James didn't give me the message. Don't you remember? When I asked him what the phone call was about, he said they didn't leave a message—and they'd ring again. He said that again this morning. And he was lying . . .

Paula is gradually beginning to understand. She moves thoughtfully below the sofa

Paula And—and have you rung your mother?
Frank Oh, yes. I rang her last night. She was as bright as a button. Nothing wrong with her at all. Whoever had rung my digs must have had a very good reason for making up a story like that.
Paula I don't understand. Why didn't James pass the message on to you?
Frank Because something happened that he hadn't bargained for. Mark had been killed. And so it was impossible for James to go ahead with his plan.

She sits on the sofa, facing him

Paula What plan?
Frank His plan to kill *me*.

A pause. Paula looks at him, astonished

Paula *You?*
Frank Yes.
Paula I—I still don't understand.
Frank I wasn't quite sure myself even last night. But then when you came back just now and told us about finding your car keys—then I knew I was right!
Paula (*puzzled*) I'm sorry. I don't quite . . .
Frank (*urgently*) The keys *were* in your car. Easy to find. But James hadn't found them. Because he hadn't *wanted* to find them. You see, he didn't want *two* cars at this house, because he had to be absolutely certain that when he gave me the urgent telephone message—and kindly, considerately lent *me* a car to go dashing off to see my poor, dying mother—it would be *his* car that I borrowed!
Paula (*slowly; realizing*) The car that he had already fixed in order to kill you and keep you quiet about what happened in the past . . .
Frank Exactly!
Paula But you'd have found out the truth. You'd have discovered that he was lying, that your mother was all right . . . (*She peters out, realizing the implications*)

Frank smiles and shakes his head

Frank No, I would never have known, because *I* would have been dead instead of Mark.

A long pause. Paula is becoming nervous and near to tears

Paula I—I can't believe it. Are you seriously suggesting that he—actually planned the whole thing? Arranging that my car was still at the garage; making sure that you came to dinner; fixing the brakes on his own car; making anonymous phone calls to your digs . . . Oh, my God! And then I—I lent the car to . . . I lent it to Mark. Oh, my God! Oh, no . . . (*She cries bitterly*)

Act II, Scene 2

Frank sits beside her and comforts her for a moment until the tears abate a little

Frank And, of course, *you* were his insurance.

She looks at him

Paula What do you mean?

Frank He knew that if the car crash that he'd arranged for me didn't look like an accident, the police would soon discover—with *his* help—that he had found out about you and Mark and all the others, and that therefore *you* had a motive for killing *him*. They would imagine that *you* had tried to kill James and that poor, unlucky Frank had been killed instead. That was his insurance. He'd have killed two birds with one stone.

She rises and moves away to the armchair

Paula No—no! I don't believe it! Nobody could be so—so devious.

Frank (*urgently*) Don't you understand? He wanted to get rid of *both* of us!

Paula No—no!—I can't believe it! I won't believe it! Not James—no!— he wouldn't do a thing like that! (*Crying helplessly*) I won't believe it ... (*She sinks into the armchair*)

Frank goes to her

Frank (*comforting her*) All right—all right, Paula. But suppose we hear it from *him*?

Paula looks up at him

Would you believe it then?

Paula But—if it *is* true—he'd never admit it.

Frank is now urgent and businesslike

Frank Look, Paula—we haven't much time. He'll be back in a minute. It's up to you.

Paula Wh—what do you mean?

Frank goes to look out of the windows to make sure that James is not coming back yet, and then returns to Paula

Frank Listen—on my way here this morning I spoke to the police.

Paula You didn't *tell* them?

Frank I told them exactly what I suspected—and how I intended to prove it. I had to be sure that James was out of the way while I spoke to you. That's why the police rang him this morning. And that's why we've got to be quick.

Paula (*bemused and frightened*) I—I don't understand ...

Frank Paula, if I'm right—James tried to kill me!

Paula (*tearfully*) But you could be wrong!

Frank Yes, but I don't think I am. The police are waiting now for a call from me.

Paula I . . . I don't know what you want me to do . . . ! (*She cries nervously, desolately*)

Frank goes to look out of the window again, then comes back to Paula

Frank Look—James wanted me dead. Right? So—tell him what he wants to hear.

She gazes at him uncomprehendingly

Paula I don't understand—I don't understand . . . !

Frank Tell him exactly what my suspicions were. That I told you, hoping to convince you—but say that you defended him angrily—we had a row—we struggled . . .

Paula And you—you . . . ?

Frank Well, there could have been an accident, couldn't there? I fell—anything!

Paula You want me to—to pretend to James that you're dead?

Frank If what I suspect is true, James won't be sorry, I can assure you.

Paula But what good will it do?

Frank Don't you see? It's our only chance! James might *say* things. Incriminating things! And the police will be listening.

Paula Wh-what do you mean?

Frank (*desperately*) At the other end of the telephone. Paula—it's our only hope!

Paula No—no, I can't—I can't do it! Anyway it wouldn't work! No! No, I won't do it!

Frank Paula—it's our only hope! (*He goes to the windows again and looks out. Then he goes quickly to the telephone and dials a number. He waits while it rings*) Inspector Jackson, please. . . . Frank Henderson. . . . Thank you. (*He puts the receiver down and goes to have another look at the windows*) He's here! He's coming up the road! (*He goes quickly back to the telephone*) Hullo? (*He waits in tense silence*) Hullo? . . . Ah—Inspector? Henderson here. . . . We're ready. He's on his way now.

Paula watches as he carefully puts the receiver down beside the telephone, and realizes what she has to do. She rises and moves away from him

Paula I can't—I can't do it!

Frank (*almost roughly*) Paula, can't you understand? Your husband may have been trying to kill both of us. And if he was—then *he* was responsible for Mark's death!

She cries

Paula—he'll be here any second!

Paula (*shivering with nerves*) But Susan—Susan—she was . . .

Frank It's all right. He's alone. The police promised he'd be alone. (*He goes to her*) Paula—*please* . . . !

Frank gives her one last appealing look, then goes quickly out to the bedrooms

Act II, Scene 2   75

Paula is shaking: frightened and emotional. She cannot control her tears and sinks on to the sofa. It is this desperate state that makes it possible for her to do what she has to do

James walks in from the garden

James Susan's coming on later. They wanted her to stay and answer some questions ... (*He sees her distressed state and goes to her quickly*) Paula—what is it? Paula—darling ...! Whatever's the matter? (*He sits beside her*)
Paula (*haltingly*) Why—why did you ...? Why did you leave me alone with him?
James What are you talking about? What's happened?
Paula You—you shouldn't have—left me—not with *him* ...
James With Frank? What do you mean? Where is he? (*He starts to go to look*)
Paula No! No—stay here—please!
James (*returning to her*) What the hell's been going on here?
Paula If you—if you hadn't left me with him—I—I would never have known ...
James Known what? Paula, darling—you must tell me! I don't understand. What's Frank been saying to you?
Paula Why didn't you *tell* me?
James Tell you? Tell you what?
Paula That you—you were paying Frank!
James Paying him?
Paula Because of what he knew ...
James I don't know what you're talking about. Paula—what the hell's Frank been saying to you?
Paula He told me everything—about the firm ...
James *Our* firm?
Paula What really happened to the firm—the things he knew about you ...
James What things about me?
Paula The things you were frightened he'd tell the police ...! (*She cries helplessly*)

He sits beside her again

James Paula, listen—you must listen!
Paula You tried to kill him, didn't you?
James Paula—for God's sake ...!
Paula You fixed the brakes on your own car!
James Don't be ridiculous! (*He rises and turns away*)
Paula You made up a story about his mother being ill—knowing he would want to go to her at once—and then you could kindly, considerately lend him your car—knowing that he was going to his death! Only it was poor Mark who drove your car—it was Mark you killed instead! (*She cries, spent and sad*)

James is very still

James (*quietly*) Oh, my God . . . (*Presently*) Where is he? Paula—where is Frank?

No reply. He starts to go to look. She rises quickly and goes to intercept him

Paula No—no! Please! You mustn't go out there!

He suspects that something has happened to Frank

James What's happened, Paula? What's happened to Frank? Paula!

She moves away towards the armchair

Paula It—it was an accident—I swear it was an accident! I didn't believe what he was saying, you see—and then—then—you must believe me! It was an accident!

James Paula—*Paula!*

She quietens a little

Frank isn't—Frank isn't dead, is he?
Paula Yes! Yes! Yes! (*She sobs hysterically and sinks into the armchair*)
James Oh, my God . . . !

A long pause. He is thinking hard. She is trying to stop the tears

Paula (*presently*) So you—you don't have to worry now, do you? You're safe—just as you wanted to be—Frank's dead and you're safe!

A pause. She is trying to control herself, the ordeal nearly over

You—you *did* try to kill Frank, didn't you?

A pause. Then he nods slowly

James Yes, Paula. I tried to kill him.

Paula cries again at hearing the truth from James. He is silent for a moment

(*Hesitantly*) He knew things about me. Things in the past. Things that happened a long time ago. Things I couldn't afford to have brought to light now. The shame—the disgrace—would ruin me. I couldn't have borne that, letting you and Susan down. (*Pause*) Frank's been blackmailing me for six months now. I had to do something. I—I couldn't just keep on paying and paying. You were right. He *did* come to see me when you were out last night. He threatened to produce his evidence and destroy me. I—I knew then that I had to do something . . .
Paula So you—you made this plan? To fix the car and—and . . . ?
James Yes. (*Pause*) Paula—Paula, darling—I couldn't possibly have known that—that Mark would . . . I couldn't possibly have known that, could I? I wish I could bring him back for you. I wish I could do that. I really do . . .

She holds on to him desperately, realizing his love for her

Frank comes in and walks down into the room

Act II, Scene 2

Frank Hullo, James . . .

James turns and sees him. He is unable to believe his eyes. He looks from Frank to Paula, realizing the trap they have made for him. He closes his eyes and moves his head slowly from side to side in horrified disbelief

James Oh, no . . . Oh, no . . . Oh, no . . .

Frank crosses slowly to the desk, picks up the telephone receiver and speaks into it

Frank All right, Inspector? . . . Yes . . . Very well. (*He replaces the receiver and looks—almost regretfully—at James*) The Inspector's on his way.

James looks back to Paula. She clings on to him. There is absolute silence, except for Paula quietly crying, as—

the CURTAIN *falls*

FURNITURE AND PROPERTY LIST

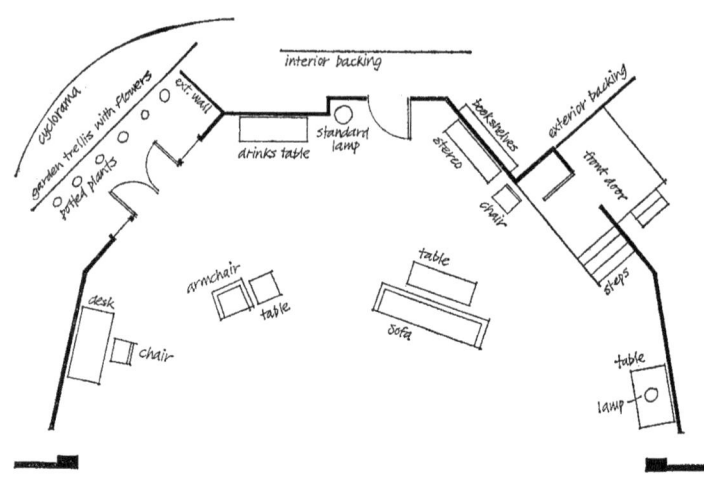

ACT I

Scene 1

On stage: Sofa. *On it:* 3 cushions
Sofa table. *On it:* cigarettes, lighter, magazines, ashtray
Armchair. *On it:* 1 cushion, **Paula**'s handbag
Armchair table. *On it:* cigarettes, lighter, ashtray, transistor radio
Desk. *On it:* telephone, writing pad, envelopes, lamp, photograph of **Susan** in frame, books, pens, etc.
Drinks table. *On it:* bottle of vodka, bottle of whisky, bottle of sherry, tonics, soda water, 6 whisky glasses, 4 vodka glasses
On shelves: books, ornaments, stereo, speakers, various L.P.s
Small table. *On it:* vase of flowers, lamp
Desk chair
Standard lamp
Carpet
Upright chair. *On it:* **Paula**'s stole

Off stage: Bunch of flowers (**Mark**)
Briefcase containing papers (**James**)
Newspaper (**James**)

Personal: **Frank:** packet of small cigars, lighter
James: wristwatch, key
Paula: wristwatch

In For The Kill

Scene 2

Strike: Used glasses
Transistor radio
Bunch of flowers

Set: Briefcase (offstage)
Paula's handbag (on armchair table)

Off stage: Plastic bag containing dress, etc. (**Susan**)

Scene 3

Off stage: Bowl of crisps (**Paula**)
Half-empty glass (**Paula**)
Full bottle of vodka (**James**)

Personal: **Frank:** handkerchief

ACT II

Scene 1

Strike: Used glasses

Off stage: Cup of coffee (**Susan**)

Personal: **Susan:** wristwatch
James: cigarettes
James: lighter

Scene 2

Set: **Paula's** handbag with car keys inside (offstage)

LIGHTING PLOT

Property fittings required: desk lamp, standard lamp, table lamp
Interior: A sitting room. The same scene throughout

ACT I. SCENE 1: A summer evening

To open: Pleasant summer sunshine

Cue 1	**James:** "... I'll expect you in half an hour, then." (Page 21)
	Fade to Black-out

ACT 1 SCENE 2: A summer evening

To open: Pleasant summer sunshine

Cue 2   Paula looks slowly back towards the window   (Page 36)
         Fade to Black-out

ACT 1 SCENE 3: A summer evening

To open: Black-out

Cue 3   As Scene opens   (Page 36)
         Fade up to lights as before

Cue 4   **James:** "I'm sorry, Paula. Mark's dead." (*Paula screams*)   (Page 42)
         Black-out

ACT II SCENE 1: Two hours later

To open: Summer evening, darker outside, lamps on

Cue 5   **Frank:** "... to drive *his* car—would be *you*."   (Page 61)
         Fade to Black-out

ACT II SCENE 2: A bright, sunny morning

To open: Bright summer sunshine

No cues

EFFECTS PLOT

ACT I

Scene 1

Cue 1	As CURTAIN rises *Noisy pop music on transistor radio*	(Page 1)
Cue 2	A moment or two later *Doorbell rings*	(Page 1)
Cue 3	After doorbell rings *Disc jockey chatter on radio, leading to quieter music*	(Page 1)
Cue 4	A moment later *Doorbell rings*	(Page 1)
Cue 5	After **Paula** enters *Doorbell rings*	(Page 1)
Cue 6	**Paula:** "I'll turn this off." *Music off*	(Page 2)
Cue 7	**Frank:** "As a matter of fact, I did." *Telephone rings*	(Page 4)
Cue 8	**Paula:** ". . . say it now while you've got the chance." *Telephone rings*	(Page 8)
Cue 9	**Frank:** ". . . at arranging an accident." *Doorbell rings*	(Page 13)
Cue 10	**James** looks at his watch *Telephone rings*	(Page 21)

Scene 2

Cue 11	As CURTAIN rises *Telephone rings*	(Page 21)
Cue 12	**James:** "We had lunch at the Club." *Telephone rings*	(Page 21)
Cue 13	**Paula** exits. Pause *Doorbell rings*	(Page 25)
Cue 14	**Paula** moves back to the house *Telephone rings*	(Page 36)
Cue 15	**Paula** looks back at the windows *Quiet, ominous music off*	(page 36)

Scene 3

Cue 16	As Lights come up *Sibelius, Symphony No. 2, on stereo*	(Page 36)

Cue 17 **Paula:** "I didn't know there was anyone here." (*She switches off stereo*) (Page 37)
Music off

Cue 18 **Frank:** "How extraordinary. What was it about?" (Page 42)
Telephone rings

ACT II

Scene 1

No cues

Scene 2

Cue 19 **Frank:** "It was your father's idea. Blame him." (Page 64)
Telephone rings

MUSIC USE NOTE

Licensees are solely responsible for obtaining formal written permission from copyright owners to use copyrighted music in the performance of this play and are strongly cautioned to do so. If no such permission is obtained by the licensee, then the licensee must use only original music that the licensee owns and controls. Licensees are solely responsible and liable for all music clearances and shall indemnify the copyright owners of the play(s) and their licensing agent, Samuel French, against any costs, expenses, losses and liabilities arising from the use of music by licensees. Please contact the appropriate music licensing authority in your territory for the rights to any incidental music.

IMPORTANT BILLING AND CREDIT REQUIREMENTS

If you have obtained performance rights to this title, please refer to your licensing agreement for important billing and credit requirements.

www.ingramcontent.com/pod-product-compliance
Ingram Content Group UK Ltd.
Pitfield, Milton Keynes, MK11 3LW, UK
UKHW021844210426
5322IPUK00022B/459